Faces From a Broken Star

Short Stories by

Gene G. Bradbury

BookWilde Children's Books Plus

Faces From a Broken Star
Short Stories
By Gene G. Bradbury
Copyright 2013 by Gene G. Bradbury

All rights reserved. No parts of this book may be reproduced or transmitted in any form or by ay means without written permission from the author.

ISBN: 978-0-9897585-2-9

Printed in the United States
By Createspace Independent Publishing Platform

Book design/prepress: Kate Weisel, weiselcreative.com

All inquiries should be addressed to

BookWilde Children's Books Plus
422 Williamson Rd.
Sequim, WA 98382

www.genegbradbury.com
Writing blog: scribblinglife.com

This book is dedicated to:
The wonderful people I've met over the years
in small town cafés and the people who serve them.

Preface

There was a time when traveling across country one might pull off the road into any small town in America and find a mom and pop café. It was a good place to order a fried chicken or roast beef dinner. In the morning farmers gathered there to compare crop prices and the weather forecast before working in the fields.

The small town café was a friendly place to stop for coffee and ask directions. Most of all, it was a gathering place for the community. The cooks and waitresses knew the regulars by name and gave a warm welcome if you were "just passing through."

A couple of years before these stories were committed to paper my wife and I drove across the United States. We searched in towns for a friendly place to eat lunch and listen for the town's pulse. To our disappointment, the once thriving café had been replaced by restaurants and convenience stores on the highway.

There's sadness and a loss for those who once enjoyed the counter seat at *The Diamond Inn* or *Ma's Diner*. The noise is different today. The atmosphere has changed. The stories in this collection recall the jangle of the bell above the door as customers entered and looked for friends. The town of Turner's Grove and The Broken Star Café are fictional. But the stories will ring true to those who remember the experience of eating a homemade cinnamon roll while the waitress behind the counter refilled your cup.

Gene G. Bradbury
April, 2014

Contents

CHAPTER ONE	After Hours	1
CHAPTER TWO	The Flute Player	7
CHAPTER THREE	First Saturday	23
CHAPTER FOUR	The Exchange	31
CHAPTER FIVE	Orlin Fingerpott's Ladies	33
CHAPTER SIX	Gilbert's Dilemma	41
CHAPTER SEVEN	The Dish Ran Away With the Spoon	47
CHAPTER EIGHT	A Figment of the Imagination	51
CHAPTER NINE	The Professor	59
CHAPTER TEN	Swimming with Victor	67
CHAPTER ELEVEN	May Your Heart Be Glad	73
CHAPTER TWELVE	Give It to the River	85
CHAPTER THIRTEEN	After the Wedding Vows	93
CHAPTER FOURTEEN	Cordon Bleu	97
CHAPTER FIFTEEN	Sara	103
CHAPTER SIXTEEN	Boston Tipps	109
CHAPTER SEVENTEEN	M. Celestine	117
CHAPTER EIGHTEEN	White Iris	123
CHAPTER NINETEEN	Twelve Lady Apostles	133
EPILOGUE	Blue Highways	139

CHAPTER ONE

After Hours

Rick Moon slumped at the counter. He fingered the black cup with the embossed blue letters: *Broken Star Café*. His burley frame, a dark paper cutout silhouetted against the dim light of the pie case. The café door was locked. The closed sign leaned against the street window. Rick glanced toward the kitchen where Doris was washing up. He turned on his stool and stared out the window at the rain. It fell like, like what? Like tears over Jakarta, he'd read somewhere.

Rick tapped his fingers on the Formica counter-top and eyed the cigarette display. He dropped two fingers into his shirt pocket and found it empty. How many times had he done that since he quit smoking? He stroked his chin and turned to face the plum colored vinyl booths, their aged cracks held together now with gray fabric tape.

"God almighty!" he said out loud. Doris would be out of a job. Hell, he hated that. He regretted closing at all. But it was time. For thirty years he'd crawled out of bed at five a.m. to unlock the door of the café and turn on lights. For twenty of those years Doris had come in at six o'clock and helloed on entering. Everything had changed.

In its heyday Turner's Grove boasted a hotel, hardware store, department store, theater, three barber shops, and a real downtown. Over the years it had shrunk to a post office, Will's Farm Supply, a bank, Ma's Grocery, a newspaper, and a few small shops. Now the Broken Star was closing. Rick had tried to sell the café. He turned back to the counter as Doris pushed through the kitchen door.

Her frazzled hair stuck to her forehead. She wore a blue apron over the white uniform. Above the pocket of her blouse her name was sown with blue thread. Rick saw she'd been crying. Doris had been a pretty, single mom twenty years ago. A small women, she bent slightly forward as if leaning over the counter to poor coffee. Rick never thought she'd last a month. Here she was on closing night.

"That's that," she said, wiping her eyes with her apron, "All spick and span."

Rick chuckled, "For what?"

"You might get a buyer yet."

"Not likely. The day of the country café is gone; it's coffee bars and bistros now. We're as extinct as the Dodo." Rick spun his cup on the counter. "We had a good run. Thirty years for me and twenty for you isn't bad."

Rick tapped the stool next to him. "Come sit down."

Out of habit Doris picked up Rick's cup and wiped the stain from the marbled gray countertop. She poured herself a cup of coffee and joined him on the other side of the counter.

He glanced toward the booths. "It's time." He waved his cup over the empty room. "If these tables could talk, they'd tell you a few stories."

"I've heard a few," said Doris.

"I'm sure you have." Rick sipped his coffee. "I won't forget Charlie Little."

"Who could forget Charlie and his bookstore?"

"We had a lot of good regulars." Rick rose from the counter and stretched his arms to the ceiling. "God, I'd like a cigarette."
Doris slid from her seat and stepped behind the counter to refill their cups. "Have you tried Life Savers?"

"Life Savers!"

"I have a friend who quit. Every time she needed a hit, she sucked on a Life Saver."

"Did it work?"

"It did for her."

Rick walked to the candy display. He opened a package of Life Savers and popped one in his mouth. "God, wouldn't you know squirrely lemon." He tried to kill the taste with a sip of coffee. "Do you have plans after closing?"

"Don't you worry, I'll be fine. My daughter and her husband live in Lincoln. I'll stay with them until I can find something else."

Rick took a Life Saver from the package and held it up to the Coca-Cola sign, "Ah, red."

He dropped the rest of the roll into his shirt pocket.

"How about you?" Doris asked.

Rick sucked the candy He was sixty now, but still looked like he could win a wrestling match like he had in high school. "You know, I've always wanted to do a road trip like that guy who wrote Blue Highways."

"You should," said Doris. "You've been nailed to this place long enough."

Rick glanced out the window. "The rain has stopped." He turned to the back booth.

"I'm going to miss this place. It's a shame." Rick rolled the Life Saver over his tongue. "We've had wonderful customers." He held a Life Saver up to the light. "You know you could fit a cigarette through the hole in one of these and smoke it down until you got to the candy."

"You're pathetic," said Doris.

He held out his cup.

Doris topped off his coffee "We've had our share of characters.

Rick glanced at the clock. "Nine thirty. I've had coffee enough to float a boat." He paused, "Let's celebrate. There's a bottle of seven-year-old scotch in the back room. What about it?"

"Why not, we'll toast to thirty years."

Rick strolled to the backroom and returned with a bottle of Jameson. "It's a gift from my son-in-law." He poured the liquid into two glasses. "Here's to thirty years of good food."

"And good customers," added Doris.

They took a healthy drink and sat quietly. The freezer's motor kicked on. A truck rumbled over the wet pavement.

"What are you thinking?" asked Doris.

"I was thinking I'm getting old and I've kept you long enough." He picked up the two glasses and started for the kitchen.

"I'll wipe down the counter before we leave," said Doris. She heard Rick running water in the kitchen. The swinging door gave a familiar flap, flap, flap as he returned.

"I'll miss that sound," said Doris.

Rick returned to the stool. "I'll miss the voices echoing through the place early in the morning."

"Listen to us." Doris suppressed a yawn.

Rick pulled the keys from his pocket. He picked up the bottle of scotch and put it in a paper bag. "I'll walk you down the street to your apartment."

Doris reached behind the counter and laid a package before Rick. "I've been working on this it seems forever."

Rick tore back the wrapper. "It's a book." He glanced at the table of contents. "What is this? Where did it come from?"

Doris grinned. "I've kept notes of some of the stories and conversations over the years. I asked a few of our customers to write down what they remembered about the Star. A friend of mine wove them together into a collection. It doesn't include everyone, but it's a good sampling of our customers."

"I'll be damned."

Pulling a Kleenex from her pocket, Doris turned toward the kitchen. "The Broken Star was important to a lot of people," she sneezed.

Rick stood up and put his arms around Doris. "Thank you."

After a long moment they stepped through the door and Rick led Doris into the night. He turned the key. The neon star in the window spread a blue light over the sidewalk as they moved down Main Street.

At home Rick flopped in his recliner. He pulled the Life Savers from his pocket, opened the book, and read the title: *Faces From a Broken Star.*

Faces From a Broken Star

CHAPTER TWO

The Flute Player

Jason Daniel pulled the Harley off the highway onto the dirt road. He slowed along the river and found a place near the bank and turned off the engine. Straddling his bike he listened to the wind tease the willow trees. Jason took a deep breath and lifted a small music case from his back.

A cool morning breeze from the river brushed his face. He closed his eyes. "Let go," he whispered. He wondered what it would be like to float to the sea? Jason slipped the flute from its case, raised it to his lips, and began to play.

He played to the river. And why not. Only too soon he would become earth to earth, ashes to ashes, dust to dust. There'd be no chance of marriage, children or career. There would be no future.

The musical notes melded with the rippling sounds of water. Jason stopped playing and soaked up the quiet. *This is how I want to live the rest of my life*, he thought.

At twenty-eight Jason had never been afraid of anything. He'd been in love. He'd graduated from a small college in the Midwest and moved on to graduate work in philosophy. He hadn't time for a full time job. He thought that would come later. Now it was too late. Three weeks ago he bought the Harley, packed a few belongings and headed west to Seattle. It was time to think about the coming months and how to make the best of them.

Jason dismounted his bike and glanced across the river. A blue heron stood perfectly still in the shallow water. Jason raised his flute and began to play. The bird lifted awkwardly into the air. He lowered his instrument and followed the prehistoric shape down river. What had Heraclitus said, "You can't step twice into the same river." He turned as a truck pulled up next to his bike. An old man in bib-overalls and red plaid shirt swung from the cab. He pulled on an old slouch hat and reached in the bed of the pick-up.

Carrying a fly-rod he approached Jason, "Mornin'." The man pointed to the bike. "Looks like you've traveled a ways."

Jason nodded.

The man reached out a hand, "Name's George Wilson. Welcome to Turner's Grove."

Jason returned the handshake. "Is there a place I can get a hot breakfast around here?"

"Just down the highway on your right you'll see the Broken Star Café. That's the spot."

Jason looked across the river, "Looks like a good day for fishing."

"We'll see, we'll see," George Wilson mumbled and walked down stream.

Jason watched him pick his way along the bank. He replaced the flute in its case and returned to his bike. He pushed the starter and rolled onto the highway.

Turner's Grove lined the highway with a string of stores on either side. Jason glanced at the twenty-five mile an hour speed sign and slowed his bike. He passed The Broken Star Café and rolled by Turner Bank, Ma's Grocery, Tiny's Tavern, and *The Turner Reporter*. Many of the store-fronts stood empty. He came to the end of town across from Will's Farm Supply.

Jason pulled to the side of the road and stared west out of town. On the right side of the road, directly ahead he saw the sign for the

City Park and Cemetery. Breakfast could wait. He passed the sign and drove up the dirt road.

Early morning fog wrapped the valley in silence. Sara Lockwood stood on her patio deck looking down the hill toward the cemetery. The sound of flute music rose out of the mist as the sun pierced the fog. The vapor parted slightly and Sara saw the man standing near the old oak. His jacket was the color of bark, and blended into the tree. She looked again to make sure he was there. A splinter of sunlight danced from the instrument. A red motorcycle was parked next to the tree, a pack strapped to the rear carrier.

Across the road sunlight splashed off the graves in the cemetery. A restful quiet had rolled over the valley. Sara took a deep breath. She had returned to Turner's Grove two years before, after her parents' deaths. After finishing a degree in fine arts, she'd accepted an offer to teach at a small Iowa college. It seemed perfect until the phone call came and changed everything.

At twenty-six she'd not expected to lose both parents. She declined the job in Iowa, moved out of her apartment in the university district, and isolated herself in the old farm house that belonged to her parents.

Sara spent the next few months walking through the cemetery and crying. She felt cheated and sank into depression. She hadn't written in all that time. Then one morning she woke with the sun in her eyes and felt something change. She couldn't explain. She poured a cup of coffee and sat on the deck to outline a story for a children's book. After coffee she moved to the Hut down the path and worked the rest of the morning. This became her routine for the next six months.

Today she stood on the deck in her white dressing gown and listened to the flute music coming from the park. A dog barked, a door slammed, a tractor engine started in a distance field.

She moved along the railing and looked down the hill toward the oak tree.

The mist parted and she could see the red motorcycle clearly.

Several gulls clamored for garbage near the picnic tables and then, rose and swept toward the graveyard. The morning folded into a rhythmic quilt of sunlight, birds, graveyard, and music.

Sara raised her birding binoculars. The man placed his instrument in a protective leather case. He strapped it to his back, mounted the bike and adjusted his helmet. For a moment all was quiet. Not a crow cawed. Not a leaf moved. The world had stopped.

She watched the flute player kick the bike into action. The roar of the engine ripped through the park. The crows scattered as the rider drove down the road leaving a trail of dust and disappeared onto the highway.

Who was he? Where was he from? Where was he going? She stared down the road. She knew she would hate herself for it; but there was no other way to satisfy her curiosity. Sara returned to the house. Dressing quickly, she was soon in the Jeep Cherokee driving through town. "This is foolish," she said out loud. She drove south and spotted the red Harley parked at The Broken Star Café.

As she opened the door Sara spotted the flute player at the counter. She moved past him to a booth near the window. If anyone found out she'd followed the man to satisfy her curiosity it would be all over town.

Doris passed by with the coffee pot. "You're getting an early start," she said.

"Things to do," Sara lied.

"Yeah, and I'm stuck for the duration. What'll you have?"

"Just coffee, for now."

Sara glanced toward the counter. The flute player was scanning the menu. She guessed he was in his late twenties. He wore faded jeans and a dark leather jacket. The flute case was strapped to his back. Sara caught bits and pieces of conversation, farmers complaining about stock prices and the weather.

She over-heard Doris say to the man, "Can I get you anything else?"

"Biscuits and gravy, please."

"You mean one of those healthy breakfasts," she chuckled. "You're not from around here."

Jason scratched his forehead, "On the road."

"Where're you headed?"

"Northwest toward the setting sun."

Doris topped off his coffee and answered the cook's bell.

Jason turned in Sara's direction. She looked into her coffee cup and brushed back her long brown hair. She was used to this and fully expected him to come to her table. He didn't. He finished his breakfast and carried the check to the cash-register. "I'm looking for some work," he said to Doris. "Do you know of anyone who needs a helping hand?"

Doris took his money, "Can you milk cows?" Jason smiled. "You might try Lyman's Dairy. They were looking for help a couple of days ago. It's the second farm going west out of town. You'll see the sign."

Jason thanked her and walked to the parking lot. Sara watched from the window as he strapped on his helmet and pulled onto the highway. Feeling rather stupid, she paid her check and drove home.

Sara paced the kitchen in her jeans and a blue pull-over sweater. She made toast, poured orange juice, and sat at the window. Sara looked over the hill toward Lyman's Dairy. She reached for the telephone after the first rang.

"It's Kate. I heard you've been out for coffee."

"God isn't anything private in this town."

Kate laughed. "Jim saw you drive away."

"I needed to get out of the house," said Sara.

"What are you doing today?" asked Kate.

Sara began pacing again.

"Are you there?

"Just thinking."

"That will get you into beaucoup trouble."

"My dad and mom have been gone two years now." Sara paused. "I miss them."

"Come for lunch at the college? I have a break after English."

"What time?"

"I'm free from one to two.

Sara hung up the phone. Kate taught at Presser Junior College in the next town. The collage library was a quiet place to work and Sara often went there for a change of scenery. She and Kate had grown up together. They'd both gone away to study and returned home. Kate finished with an English Lit major and Sara with a Master's Degree in Fine Arts.

Sara showered, changed clothes and stepped down the path toward the hut her parents had built among the trees. They'd been avid bird watchers and enjoyed the quiet woods. After their death Sara converted the hut into a writer's studio. She loved the way the birds danced on the roof and how the rain dripped from the trees.

This morning she started a fire in the wood stove. The hut normally gave her a sense of being far away, but not this morning. The quiet usually wrapped around her like a security blanket, but today she found herself doodling motorcycles on a note pad. She needed to concentrate. Why couldn't she settle down? It was strange. She didn't even know the man and yet...

She stared out the window. *God, what's wrong with me?* She wadded up the page from the note pad and threw it into the waste basket. Sara turned on the computer and called up: *The Bashful Dragon Goes to School*.

At 12:30 Sara stuffed the hard copy of the children's story in a folder and drove to Presser. She parked in the student lot and entered the cafeteria just as Kate arrived. "How about a salad and split a veggie sandwich?" said Kate.

They found a table near the window.

"So, did you get some work done?" asked Kate.

"A little, I don't have a lot of experience with dragon schools. I'll do some editing in the library."

"Let's get back to your problem," said Kate.

"My problem, I don't have a problem."

"Alright, let's talk about your loneliness then."

"Oh that. It's nothing. It comes and goes."

"You need someone."

"You can stop right there," said Sara. "I know where this is going."

"I'm just trying to help.

"Let's talk about something else."

"Okay," said Kate. "There is a new teacher in the science department. He's very good looking and single."

Sara shot her a nasty look. "Stop," she said. "I'm not interested. I have plenty to keep me busy. I don't need a man in my life" She looked past Kate. "Oh, god, there he is!"

"Who?" asked Kat.

"The flute player," Sara whispered.

"The What?"

"It's nothing. Forget it."

Kate turned and eyed the man standing at the door.

"Some guy I saw at the Star this morning. He rides a Harley."

Kate turned back, "Very nice. Are you interested?"

"Oh, stop it. I'm a writer. Writers are curious."

"So when will the book be ready?"

"I have a long way to go," said Sara.

"Ah, well then, I'll return to work. I must make the Romantic Poets live." Kate picked up her dishes, placed them in a container. She walked past the table where Jason sat, turned at the door and gave Sara a thumbs up.

Sara picked up her folder and walked through the campus to the library. She found her usual table and unpacked her bag. It was time to concentrate.

"Excuse me." Sara turned to find the flute player standing behind her. "I saw you in the cafeteria and thought you might work here."

Sara brushed her hair back and managed, "No, my friend does."

"I didn't see anyone at the desk and I want to ask about checking out books."

"You might try the office." Sara pointed to a door across the room.

"Thanks," he said and walked away.

Sara sat down and pulled a folder from her bag. "This is so weird," she mumbled. "I feel like I'm in some kind of time-warp." She turned to the Bashful Dragon.

In a few minutes Jason passed her with a stack of books and sat at a table a few feet away. An hour later he took a book from the stack and left the others on the table. He smiled as he passed her table.

"Did you find what you were looking for?" asked Sara.

"I think so."

"I saw you at the Broken Star in Turner's Grove. I don't want to be nosy, (Yes she did), but did you find work?"

He laughed. "It is a small town. Yes, I'm working at the dairy for a few days."

"I live on the next place south up cemetery road." She hesitated. "I'm having a few friends over tomorrow night. If you'd like to drop by, you're invited."

He hesitated. "Thanks, I'll think about it," he said and walked off.

"I can't believe I did that," Sara said to herself.

Sara gathered her pages. On her way out she thumbed through the stack of books the man left on the next table. "Recent Research on Ten Incurable Diseases," she repeated. *They were medical books. Was he a medical student?*

Sara left the library and returned to Kate's office. "How was class?" she said, finding Kate at her desk.

"We discussed the *Rhyme of the Ancient Mariner*. Did Coleridge write it by himself? Did Wordsworth contribute? If so, should he have been given credit?"

"Ah," said Sara, "into the nitty-gritty of the Romantic Poets."

"Did you get some work done?"

"A weird thing happened. That man, the one in the cafeteria, was in the library." Sara walked to the window and looked out on the quad. Kate raised an eyebrow, "and…"

"And nothing," Sara paused, "well, almost nothing. I did a stupid thing. I invited him to a gathering of friends I'm having tomorrow night."

Kate laughed. "What gathering?"

Sara turned from the window. "Exactly," said Sara. "What gathering?" She rolled her eyes. "God, can you help me call a few people? I don't know why I did it. I just…"

"Well, I have a Yoga class and I'm not god; but I'll see what I can do," said Kate.

"What Yoga class?"

"Just kidding, I'll come and bring Jim and call Melody and Karla."

"Let's say six o'clock. I'll have munchies and drinks."

"I can bring chips and dip and a couple of bottles of wine," offered Kate.

"Thanks, I don't know why I do these things."

"I do," said Kate. "You're hopeful."

Sara frowned. "Thanks doctor, but wrong diagnosis."

The next day Sara went to the Hut in the morning and spent the afternoon getting ready for the party. Guests began arriving at six o'clock. Sara poured wine moving in and out of conversations.

"This was a surprise," said Jim. "I didn't hear about it until last night."

"A last minute idea," explained Sara. "It's such beautiful weather this time of year. Why not take advantage of it?"

"Right you are," he said.

Sara wandered to the outside deck where Melody and Karla sat talking.

"You have such a great view," said Karla. "I've always envied you this place."

Sara peered down the dirt road past the cemetery. "I like it." She glanced at her watch. "More wine?"

Kate stepped behind Sara and whispered, "He's not coming, is he?"

"Who?" asked Sara.

Kate laughed. "You know who, your invitee."

Sara turned as a motor shifted gears up the hill. The headlight of the red Harley flicked over the grave stones as it passed the cemetery. Jason pulled into the drive and Sara went to the open the door., "You made it," she said.

"I needed a break and can't pass up free food. My name is Jason, by the way."

"I'm Kate. Come in, I'll introduce you to my friends."

They walked through the living room onto the deck. Sara introduced Jason to everyone and asked, "Beer or wine?"

"Red wine, please." Jason took a seat at a table and fielded the usual questions. "I'm just passing through. Yes, staying a few days to work at the dairy over the hill. No, never been here before. No, I'm not married." He settled in and listened to the conversation swimming around him. The talk and laughter increased as the evening grew late and wine bottles emptied. Guests started leaving about ten o'clock. Jason stood to leave and Sara walked Jason to his bike.

"Thanks for coming."

"Thanks for inviting." He started his bike, waved goodbye and rode down the hill.

Kate said from the doorway, "He doesn't say much, does he?"

"He's quiet," said Sara.

They returned to the deck and sat in the dark. "He's almost too quiet," said Kate. "Maybe he's hiding something."

Sara stared into the night.

"Maybe he's on the F.B.I's most wanted list," suggested Kate.

"Oh, stop it. He's thoughtful, that's all."

Kate sat up, "I hear music?"

The faint sound of the flute drifted up the hill. Sara had forgotten the flute. She strained to listen.

"Where's it coming from," asked Kate?

"Near the cemetery," said Sara. "He's played there before. She yawned. Do you mind if I call it a day? It's late and tomorrow is a work day." Sara hugged Kate. "Thanks for helping me out tonight."

"It was fun. Let me know the next time you invite a strange man for a party."

Sara smiled and walked Kate to the door.

Four days went by. Sara worked in the Hut. She was pasting together a picture book dummy when she heard the Harley come up the road. Sara walked up the path to find Jason at her door.

"I'm afraid no one's home," she called.

Jason turned and smiled. "I thought you might like to go for a ride. It's my way of thanking you for the party."

Sara eyed the bike. "I don't have a helmet."

"I borrowed an extra." He paused. "It's completely safe. I'm a good driver."

Sara hesitated. "It's just that I've never been on one before."

"I won't take any chances."

"All right, give me a minute to change."

"I'll wait here," he said.

When she returned Sara suggested they go to the Blue River. Jason steered past the cemetery and onto the highway. He followed Sara's directions to dirt cut off and parked next to the water. They removed their helmets and placed them on the handle-bars.

Sara brushed out her hair. "That was fun," she said.

"You weren't afraid," he asked?

"Not really. Why?"

"I thought you might be. It was the way you were holding on."

"Sorry."

"No need to be." Jason switched his flute case from the front of his jacket to the back.

"Let's walk this way," said Sara. There's a place I love." As they hiked along the river Jason took a deep breath, "You can actually breathe and hear the birds."

"You don't have birds where you're from?" asked Sara.

"We have citified crows and statue pigeons that desecrate the park benches."

They came to a bend in the river. "We're here," said Sara, "the place of still waters."

"You're a Bible reader then," said Jason. "He makes me lie down by still waters."

"My parents brought me up to be a spiritual person."

Jason stared across the river. "Do you believe in life after death?"

Sara turned to him. "You're Mr. Serious today."

"I suppose," he said. "How would you like some music?" Jason unzipped the instrument case and lifted the flute.

Sara watched wet his lips and began to play. When he stopped, she said, "It fits somehow. It's an instrument for the outdoors."

"You're right," agreed Jason. "Do you play an instrument?"

"I play piano very badly."

Jason lifted the instrument to his mouth and played again. After a few minutes he stopped and listened. "This place is so perfect." He paused. "I have to leave in a couple of days. It's too bad. I like it here."

Sara focused on the river. "Do you have to go?"

"Yes, I have things to do in Seattle."

"Can you come to dinner tomorrow night?"

"I shouldn't," he said. "Let me think about it. My life is on hold right now."

"On hold," said Sara.

"I can't get involved with someone."

"That's fine. Just come for dinner. Now, I must get back to work."

"What kind of work?"

"I'm writing a children's book."

Jason smiled. "What a lovely job."

"It is," said Sara. "It allows me to think childish things."

"Ah, the Apostle Paul."

Sara laughed. "I guess some of my mother rubbed off on me."

They left the river and Jason dropped Sara at her house. She handed him the helmet.

"Come at six."

Jason nodded and started the engine.

The following night Jason sat on the deck with a glass of wine. He stretched out in his chair with his hands behind his head. Sara came from the kitchen and set a salad before him.

"This is nice of you," he said.

"I get tired of eating alone," said Sara.

Jason spooned honey-mustard dressing over his salad. "This is a great place."

"I grew up here. My parents and grandparents are buried in the cemetery." She pointed down the hill. Sara took a bite of salad. "I have almost everything I need."

"How long have your parents been gone?"

"Three years. They were killed in a train-car accident." She paused. "I miss them."

"Tell me about your writing."

"There isn't much to tell unless you like shy dragons that go to preschool."

Jason smiled. "Were you a dragon in preschool?"

"That's perceptive of you. I was a preschool drop-out. But that's another story. I enjoy writing. I'm lucky. My parents left me this house and enough to live on for a while."

"You said you have almost everything you need. Almost isn't everything."

Sara set her fork down and sat up. "Who does?" She looked over the valley. "I suppose I don't want to go through life alone, if that's what you mean."

Jason nodded. "You shouldn't."

"I just haven't met the right person," said Sara. "I'm good for now."

Jason finished his salad.

"I'll get dinner out of the oven. I hope you like fresh fish."

"I do. Can I help?"

"No, I just have to put it on a platter. She left the table and returned with a steaming plate of trout, rice, and asparagus.

"Looks great," said Jason. "Do you eat often at the Broken Star?"

"Occasionally." Sara picked up her fork. "You know my friends think you're mysterious?"

"Do they?" Jason took a bite of fish. "Well, it's not intentional. I'm a pretty private person."

"I know," said Sara. "Your life is on hold."

Jason laid down his fork and sipped his wine. "I'm sorry. I don't mean to be mysterious. There are things I can't talk about now."

"Sorry, it's really none of my business." Sara slid her chair back. "But when someone rides up my road on a red Harley and plays the flute in my valley, I get curious."

"My road. My valley," Jason laughed. "Fair enough. Now, will you show me YOUR studio?"

"I planned to have coffee there. You can carry dessert."

Jason followed Sara to the kitchen and out the back door to the path leading to the hut. He paused as Sara unlocked the door.

"I like it already."

"It's home. Other than Jeffery, the resident mouse you are the only visitor I've allowed here in weeks."

"I guess that makes me special. Will I meet Jeffery?"

"Hopefully not." Sara took the pie from him and laid it on the small work table. "I could write in the house. I like to get away from the phone and interruptions."

"Like people banging on your door?"

Sara smiled. "Down here I'm surrounded by woods where dragons live." She poured the coffee made earlier in the day and dished up pie. They carried their plates to the chairs under the trees.

"Where did you learn to play the flute?"

"Wonderful apple pie," said Jason. "When I was a kid I wanted to play an instrument. My friends were taking guitar lessons and trying to be The Rolling Stones. I choose the flute."

"Isn't that an unusual instrument for a guy?"

Jason laughed. "Have you ever heard of Jean Pierre Rampal or James Galway?"

"Of course, but what teenager listens to them?"

"I did. I'll admit there may be some gender prejudice against the flute, but I wanted something that I could play by myself. We lived in the city and the only place to be alone was in my room or at a nearby park. I choose the flute because I can carry it anywhere."

Sara watched a squirrel scurry up a nearby tree. She turned to face Jason. "The first time I heard you play was under the oak tree across from the cemetery. It seemed perfect. Do you often stop and play when you travel?"

"If I find the right place I pull off the road and find holtzvol."

Sara raised her eyes, "Holtzvol?"

"It's the Navajo word for harmony."

"Now who's spiritual?" Sara smiled at him. "But you're not in harmony. You're on hold."

"That's true. But at this moment I'm perfectly satisfied in body and mind and need to get back."

"It's still early."

Jason brushed back his hair. He stood and took her plate. "I'm leaving early tomorrow. I'll carry these back and stay long enough to help with dishes."

"It's not necessary."

They threaded their way to the house and set the dishes on the kitchen table. Sara followed Jason to his bike. He strapped on his helmet and reached into his saddlebag. "Would you mind returning this to the library when you go? It will save me a stop tomorrow."

Sara took the book and glanced at it.

"So you're a baseball fan."

"At times. Thanks for a wonderful evening. I'll send you a post card from Seattle."

Sara stepped back as he started the bike. She returned to the kitchen and set the dishes on the counter along with the book. She undressed and thought she heard music. It was the flute. Sara threw on her robe and walked to the deck. The darkness hid Jason, but the music rolled up the hill like fresh air and surrounded her. *It's the perfect instrument for outdoors,* she thought.

The music stopped. All was quiet again. In a moment the sound of the engine struck the night. Sara watched the bike's taillights disappear down the road. She returned to the kitchen to turn off the lights. The book lay on the table. *The Luckiest Man: The Life and Death of Lou Gehrig*, by Jonathan Eig.

At two o'clock in the morning Sara started awake. She slid from bed and ran to the deck overlooking the cemetery. It all fit, the medical books, Lou Gehrig, my life is on hold.

Sara sat down and looked toward the graveyard. Tears dropped down her eyes. It all made sense. It was so unfair.

CHAPTER THREE

First Saturday

Jennifer woke, rubbed her eyes and groaned, "Dear God, it's the first Saturday and another aunts day out." She poked Freeman, "Wake up Freeman. It's the first Saturday of June."

"It can't be," he mumbled. "I thought we'd drive to Turner's Grove and have a leisurely breakfast at the Broken Star Café this morning."

"We can't. We promised May and the others a picnic at Turner Lake. Aunt May will already have called the others."

May, who lived with Freeman and Jennifer, referred to them as, "The Keepers," as if she lived in the zoo. This morning she sat in the kitchen in a loose fitting smock and flip-flops, excited about the day.

Freeman and Jennifer were to act as their transporters, chaperones, and motivators. In cold weather they might go to the Star for lunch. But summer had arrived and the aunts had asked for a picnic.

Freeman shaved, dressed, and stumbled into the kitchen. "Good morning, Aunt May."

"Good morning, dear." Aunt May speared a healthy bite of griddle-cakes. May was the youngest of four sisters, and maliciously called "The Wider" by the others.

"You'd better eat," she said. "You'll need plenty of energy to keep up with us today."

"My mother said the same thing," replied Freeman.

"Yes, dear, I do miss your mother. She was the first of us to go." May rolled a slab of pancake through the syrup. "Now about today, dear, you know Muriel is a hypochondriac. She will complain of being near the water and will wear three sweaters even in June."

Freeman nodded his head.

"And Myra, my God, you know Myra? She'll talk politics and rant on about the environment till you turn to butter. We'd best be prepared. Now, dear, how about the picnic, you *are* bringing a large basket."

Freeman smiled. "Yes, Aunt May, Jennifer made it up yesterday."

May clapped her hands in delight. "Then all shall be well."

An hour later May folded herself into the middle seat of the van. Freeman swung into the driver's side after placing the picnic basket and blankets in the back. Jennifer climbed into the passenger seat and stared straight ahead. She clasped her book to her chest as if it were a life preserver. She had chosen *In the Presence of the Enemy*, by Elizabeth George. She smiled. It would fortify her against the battle of the aunts. Jennifer loved the aunts. They were certainly characters. But she knew a headache promised by the end of the day.

The first stop was Muriel's high-rise apartment on the south side of Presser. Freeman hoped aunt number two would be waiting for them at the curb. But he knew she would be peering out the window waiting for him to call on the intercom, climb the stairs, and take the elevator to her floor. Freeman parked in the passenger loading zone.

"Why can't she come down by herself?" grumbled May from the middle seat.

Freeman shut the van door and mounted the steps to the apartment. He pressed the intercom.

"Hello, who is it?" asked the suspicious voice.

"It's me, Freeman, Aunt Muriel. Do you want to come down?"

"No, sonny, you'd better come up and get me."

Freeman never understood why Aunt Muriel called him sonny, but then, why not. May called him dear and Myra, Maggie's Boy. The door buzzed allowing him entrance. Freeman rode the elevator to the sixth floor. He knocked and heard Muriel's voice, "Who is it?" Freeman sighed, thinking, it's going to be a long day. Out loud he said, "It's me, Aunt Muriel." He heard the first lock give way, then a second and a third. The door opened a crack and Muriel peered into the hallway.

"It is you," she said.

They made their way safely down the stairs to the van and Muriel said, "Now, lock us in, won't you, sonny?"

Jennifer smiled and opened her book. Freeman rolled his eyes and drove away.

Myra's cottage was north of The Lake. She raised chickens for the eggs and tended an organic vegetable garden. The sign on the gate read, "Free Tibet." Freeman drove through the gate and parked. He strolled up the brick walk and rang the bell.

The door opened and Myra said through the screen door, "Oh, it's Maggie's Boy. I was watching the news. Can you believe the violence in the world? We should never be at war in those places. What good is it doing?"

"Aunt Myra, are you going with us today?" Freeman asked.

"Oh, yes, I hadn't forgotten. Just let me get my things." She disappeared into the bedroom. Freeman glanced over the room stacked with magazines and newspapers. *U.S. News and World Report* and *Newsweek* lay near Myra's reading chair. Myra emerged from the bedroom and asked, "Did Jennifer pack any vegetarian food for the picnic?"

"Yes," said Freeman "She didn't forget."

They made their way past the bumper sticker on the door declaring "Peace is Patriotic."

In the van preliminary kisses were exchanged and Freeman drove the remaining mile to Turner Lake. He parked near the path that led to the picnic area. The aunts piled out and shuffled down the path in their flip-flops. Freeman raised an eyebrow again and Jennifer smiled. They carried the picnic basket, blankets, umbrella, and lawn chairs to the river.

"My, this looks nice," said May.

"Not too close to the water, now," instructed Muriel. "You know how damp it can get. You might catch a chill."

"Oh hush," said May. "It's a beautiful day and you're not going to catch a chill. Maybe you should quit worrying and try to enjoy yourself for a change."

Muriel stabbed her with the first murderous look of the day. Grabbing a folding chair, she stomped to a warm spot in the sun. "That's what I get for being nice," she shouted back. Muriel pulled her sweaters around her, straightened her large straw hat, and began rubbing sun screen on her skin still exposed.

Freeman arranged blankets and chairs. Jennifer spread the table cloth on the picnic table and set the basket at one end. Myra, her hands on hips, drummed the sand with one tennis-shoe.

"Just look at this beach. People are such slobs. You'd think they would pick up after themselves." She pulled her baseball cap down and began putting trash in a plastic bag.

May wandered over to the table and opened the picnic basket.

"Aunt May, you just had breakfast," said Freeman.

"That was some time ago, dear. I'm just thinking ahead."

"We'll eat in a little while," offered Jennifer and opened her book. *Helen kicked off her shoes inside the front door of the building in which she lived. She whispered, "Mercy," at the sweet sensation of feet being released from agonizing servitude to the god of fashion.*

Jennifer closed the book and looked over the lake. She thought about the aunts' daily battles with gluttony, illness and social issues. She slipped on her sunglasses. "Freeman, I'm going for a walk."

Freeman watched her slide away, admiring her slim figure in shorts and halter-top.

Jennifer heard May call after her, "Don't be gone too long, dear, it's almost lunch time." She passed Muriel huddled in her chair. Further down the beach Jennifer caught up with Myra bending over a beer can. "It's a beautiful day," she said.

Myra raised her head and nodded. "Would you like to take a trash bag with you?"

"No, thank you. I'm walking for enjoyment."

After an hour May began to pace. She looked over at Muriel who had turned her back on everyone. Myra approached, dragging a full bag of trash over the sand.

"Just look at this," she said as she neared the picnic table. "I'm going to the recycle bins."

Muriel turned and called from her chair, "You'd better wear gloves."

When Jennifer returned she found the aunts waiting at the table and Freeman setting out plates of chicken and sandwiches.

"My, look at the flies," said Muriel. "It's enough to make you sick, all those tiny feet pitter-pattering on the potato salad." She wrapped a ham sandwich carefully in a paper napkin. "How can you eat dead pigs?" asked Myra. "Do you know how chickens and pigs are crowded into buildings and never see the light of day? It's disgusting."

"Freeman, would you like a leg?" asked Jennifer.

"Maybe later," Freeman smiled.

May glared at Myra, gulped her drink, devoured a third boiled egg and burped. "Excuse me," she said.

"You eat too fast," said Muriel. "Someday you're going to choke on a chicken bone."

"Eggs don't have bones," barked May.

"Muriel, has anyone ever told you that you're a P E S T, pest?"

Muriel glared at May. "At least I don't eat like a P I G, pig, and look like a H I P P O, hippo," rejoined Muriel.

"You're both sad cases," said Myra. "Neither of you have an ounce of social sense. You never have. You're too wrapped up in yourselves to care anything about the planet."

Jennifer sighed and watched the other sisters pin Myra with evil eyes. At the same time she became aware of squawking ducks over the lake.

"Well, it's true," Myra said.

"I don't have to put up with this," cried May." Its abuse, that's what it is. And it's nothing new. As the oldest, you've always abused your younger sisters. It's not fair."

May grabbed a chicken leg and flip-flopped down the beach.

"Wait, I'll come too," offered Muriel. "I know when I'm not wanted."

Myra took her drink and strolled in the opposite direction.

Left by themselves, Jennifer moved her bare foot under the table and stoked Freeman's foot. He looked up and smiled. "I'll have that leg now."

A few minutes later May returned to the picnic table in a funk. "Where's Muriel?" asked Freeman.

"I hope she's drowned," huffed May. "She's a witch in sheep's clothing."

"You mean a fox," corrected Freeman. "A fox in sheep's clothing."

"Fox, witch, devil, bitch, it's all the same to me."

"Why can't the three of you get along?" asked Jennifer. "It's this way every month. Don't you get tired of arguing?"

May paused. "To tell the truth, we haven't gotten along since Maggie died. She held us together. We never argued when Maggie was alive."

"I know." Jennifer reached out and touched May's hand. "Maybe if…," she began.

Muriel stomped past the table. "I'm cold. I'll be in the van." She limped off in the direction of the parking lot.

May picked a pudding cup from the basket. "I think our July outing should be to a nice restaurant."

Myra raised an eyebrow, but didn't say anything.

"We may have to skip our July outing," said Freeman. "Jennifer and I are planning a trip of our own that month."

Jennifer closed the basket and smiled at Freeman.

"At least the beach is a lot cleaner since we came," said Myra.

When they reached the car, Muriel was asleep in the back seat. "She looks so peaceful," said Freeman.

"And healthy," said Jennifer.

The drive back to Myra's and then to town was quiet. Each aunt turned to their own window. They dropped Aunt Myra at her cottage. "Don't forget Wednesday at the Broken Star," she said to the others and closed the door.

Freeman escorted Aunt Muriel up the elevator to her apartment and listened as she slid the locks into place. At home May returned to her room without speaking.

Puzzled, Freeman smiled. Exhausted, Jennifer sank into a chair on the patio. As Freeman handed her a class of wine she said, "You know I've always known that too many aunts can spoil a picnic."

Faces From a Broken Star

CHAPTER FOUR

The Exchange

George Wilson stopped by the Broken Star Café to fill his thermos. He arrived at the Blue River and poured himself a cup of coffee. He opened his pocket watch to the engraving: *Hooked line and sinker on our wedding day, Love Virginia, June 10, 1920.*

Had it really been sixty years? George closed the watch and corked the thermos. He picked up his fly-pole and strolled downstream to a spot across from the willow stand where shadows danced and the water ran deep. George pulled a black leather fly case from his fishing vest. He opened the case and smiled. He would catch no fish today.

George sat on a log and glanced over the water. He recalled his second year at the University. Mrs. Sutton rented him a room and provided evening meals. Her daughter, Virginia, was nineteen, beautiful and sophisticated. He was a shy, bumbling farm boy from Turner's Grove.

In his second year George managed to ask Virginia to the movies. During the following weeks Virginia's mother began turning dinner conversation to the topic of marriage. George felt the idea drop into his mind like a caddis fly on water. He thought if he asked Virginia and she said yes, it would be like landing a 20-inch Rainbow Trout. But George also knew what it was to hook a big one and watch it get away.

One night after dinner Virginia's mother handed them each a gift. "Don't open them now," she said mysteriously. "Open them tonight before you go to bed."

George and Virginia placed the gifts in their rooms and went for a walk. They returned at ten o'clock. George put on his pajamas and unwrapped his present. He knew from the size that it was a black leather fly-case. He opened it and frowned. Inside he found needles, thread and buttons. "It's a sewing kit," he said out loud. George pulled on his robe and stepped down the hall to Virginia's door. She opened it wearing a light negligee. "I believe this is yours," she said, holding out an identical case.

They exchanged the cases and smiled. Virginia reached out and pulled George into the room. George took her in his arms, "Was this a trick of your mother's?"

Virginia pushed him away. "George Wilson, how can you think my mother would stoop to trickery to get you to marry me?"

"Will you marry me?" George asked.

That was 60 years ago, today, June 10th. George packed his fishing gear and returned home. Virginia heard the truck on the gravel drive. She grabbed the fly-case from her sewing basket and ran to the door.

George smiled at her. "I think this is yours," he said, pulling the sewing kit from his vest.

"Fish weren't biting on buttons today."

"And this is yours," she said, handing him his fly-case. "Sewing wasn't so good either." Virginia pulled him through the doorway as she had sixty years before.

"I'm wondering," said George. "Did you deliberately plant your sewing case in my vest to remind me of our anniversary?"

"George Wilson. Do you think I would stoop to trickery just to get you to remember our anniversary?"

George took her in his arms and whispered, "Like mother, like daughter. Happy anniversary."

CHAPTER FIVE

Orlin Fingerpott's Ladies

Orlin Fingerpott took his morning coffee break at the Broken Star Café. He walked the short distance from Ma's Grocery and strutted through the door like a chanticleer. He wore a yellow sweat shirt, jeans, and topped off his five-foot, six-inch frame with an orange baseball cap. Rick Moon, the owner of the Broken Star, described Orlin as a stubby yellow pencil with a good eraser. Orlin climbed on a stool near the cash register to watch Doris work the counter.

Rick called from the service window. "How are the pigeons, Orlin?" Orlin flicked a feather off his shirt and checked his shoes.

"It's too late for that," said Rick.

"Sorry, Mr. Moon." Orlin paused, a large grin on his face. "The pigeons are fine, but it looks like a lot of weather out today."

"Weather's like whiskers on a bobcat," said Rick. "You notice it most when it's upon you."

"Coffee, Orlin?" asked Doris.

"That'd be nice, Ms. D."

"You're cheery today."

"I'm excited. Bernice, my newest lady pigeon, flew to Presser for the first time. My friend, Burley Early, will be sending her back today."

"Hooray for Bernice."

"I have five carriers now. Burley and me don't use any telephone. We think homing pigeons are better. Mrs. Story lets me keep my pigeon coop in back of the boarding house." Orlin swallowed the last of his coffee. "Well, I'm off to stock shelves. See you tomorrow, Ms. D."

"Enjoy all that weather, Orlin," yelled Rick from the kitchen.

After work Orlin raced to the dovecote. He searched inside, but Bernice hadn't returned. He lifted his cap and scratched his head. Orlin searched the sky. It opened to him like an empty hand. He climbed the stairs to his room and peered out the upstairs window toward Presser. *It's early yet*, he thought.

At six o'clock Orlin checked the dovecote again. He prepared Hester, his most reliable lady, to carry a message to Burley. "Burley, did you send Bernice?" He placed the small cylinder on Hester's back and lifted her into the air.

Early the next morning he found Hester in the dovecote with a message, "Sent Bernice yesterday. 3 p.m. Burley.

"Blast it!" swore Orlin. At ten o'clock he trudged to the Broken Star and dropped onto a stool.

"Good morning, Orlin."

"Not so good, Ms. D. Bernice is missing,"

"She's lost?"

"I guess." He held out his cup. "Sometimes pigeons fly off course if they're hungry."

The kitchen door swung open. A young girl began putting dishes under the counter. Orlin ran his hand through his hair. Doris said, "This is Rick's niece, Abigail. She flew in from Minneapolis."

Orlin slid from his stool spilling his coffee. "Nice to meet you, Ms. Abigail."

Abigail shook Orlin's hand and quickly wiped her hand on her apron. She pushed back through the swinging door to the kitchen. Orlin took his stool and Doris refilled his coffee cup.

"She's beautiful, alright."

Doris glanced toward the kitchen. "Who are you talking about?"

Orlin blushed. "Oh, Bernice," said Orlin. "I picked her out of all the birds at the Southern Nebraska Homing Pigeon Association Conference last year."

"She's special, then," said Doris.

Orlin got up to leave. "She is. Her flying away is a tragedy, that's what it is," he said as he opened the door.

"I hope you find her. She sounds precious," yelled Doris.

"She's one of my ladies," said Orlin, chancing a last glimpse toward the kitchen.

At Ma's Grocery Orlin tried stocking shelves. He mixed the onion soup cans with the tomato soup cans and chicken soup with the bean soup. His mind seemed as jumpy as a grasshopper. He thought of Bernice lost in some field or worse yet, eaten by coyotes. Then his brain made a U-turn, and he whispered, "That Abigail is pretty as a prize bird."

Orlin raced home to check the dovecote. There was no Bernice. That night Orlin tossed and turned in bed. He woke Sunday morning, shaved, put on fresh jeans, and walked to the Star.

"You're early this morning," said Doris. "Has Bernice returned?"

Orlin shook his head. "She's somewhere alright. She's my sweetest lady. I'm off to do a search." He flicked a look toward the kitchen. "Where's Abigail?"

"She's learning the counter today."

"She'll make a fine waitress," said Orlin.

"You're an expert on waitresses, are you?" asked Doris.

Orlin blushed. Abigail was the prettiest thing he'd seen since finding Bernice at the Pigeon Association meeting. She reminded Orlin of a sleek bird on the wing. He was sure her skin must be as soft as feathers. And her dark grey eyes were a dove's eyes for sure and froze him in place. *What a prize*, he thought.

The kitchen door flapped back and forth and Abigail appeared, holding a tray of cups.

"Who's Bernice?" she asked.

"Good morning, Ms. Abigail. Bernice is my lost pigeon."

"Did she get out?" asked Abigail.

"No, she's a carrier pigeon," said Orlin. "But carriers fly off course sometimes to find water or food. Two years ago Shirley got lost. We found her feathers near Henry and Florence's farm."

"I'm sorry," said Abigail.

"Bernice is registered and banded with an identification ring. If someone finds her she might be returned."

Abigail wiped down the counter. "I hope you find her."

"She's one of my ladies," said Orlin.

"So you're a ladies man," Abigail laughed.

Orlin covered his face with his baseball cap. "I wouldn't say that," he said in muffled words.

"Well, I know how it feels to lose a pet."

"You do?"

"The coyotes got Sable, my favorite cat."

"Hawks and coyotes love it around here," said Orlin.

Abigail walked to table number three to refill coffee cups. Returning she asked, "What kind of name is Fingerpott?"

Orlin stared out the window. A bubble formed in his head with the words, Abigail Fingerpott. He blinked and the bubble popped.

"What kind of name is Fingerpott?" repeated Abigail.

"I'm sorry," said Orlin. "Fingerpotts settled here years ago. Most of them moved away, except me, of course. I'm still here."

"I can see that," said Abigail. She poured him more coffee and moved along the counter. Orlin, embarrassed, covered his eyes with his hand. He imagined the dovecote too, but instead of Bernice, Abigail waited for him to open the door.

Orlin sprang from his stool and dropped some change on the counter. Without saying goodbye, he left the café and shuffled toward home.

Didn't the English call women, birds? Bernice and Abigail were both lovely, soft feathered birds. In the yard he heard cooing from the dovecote and recalled Abigail's soft voice, "So you're a ladies man."

The September sky threatened rain. Orlin packed a peanut-butter and jelly sandwich and headed across the fields toward Turner Lake. He lifted his eyes to the sky, hoping to see Bernice. Clouds moved swiftly, spreading shadows over the ground.

There wasn't much hope of finding Bernice. He hoped with a lover's heart for the impossible. Orlin dreaded finding her feathers and mutilated body. He trudged past the backs of the town shops into the fields beyond.

In Henry and Florence's pasture Orlin searched the ground for clues. Near a fallen log he found scattered feathers, but they were the wrong color. Maybe a goose or gull, he thought. Orlin tramped through the woods until he grew hungry. He straddled a log to eat his sandwich.

After lunch Orlin turned toward Tyrell William's cabin at Turner Lake. Tyrell, who everyone called the Professor, was the only black man in Turner's Grove. As Orlin approached the cabin he saw the Professor sitting on a stump near the water. "Professor!" he yelled.

Tyrell stood and waved toward his visitor. "Mr. Orlin, here you are at my little place."

"I am, Professor."

"Out for a Sunday stroll, I'll bet."

"Not exactly," said Orlin.

"Well, I'm mighty pleased you've come this way. I go to town on Tuesday and was trying to figure a way to bring something back I think belongs to you."

Orlin stopped in his tracks. He stared at the Professor. "You found Bernice."

"If Bernice is a pigeon, I did indeed."

Orlin bent over, his hands on his knees and sucked in his breath. He didn't want to cry in front of the Professor, but he couldn't stop the tears.

Tyrell turned politely toward the lake.

"Is she okay, Professor?" Orlin finally managed.

"She's fine. I gave her water and food."

Orlin sighed, "Thank you, Professor. I've been so worried. She's my most beautiful lady."

"I figured as much. I found her not far from here lying in tall grass. She seemed exhausted, didn't even object when I picked her up. I brought her inside near the fire. We've been friends ever since. You come on in now and see for yourself."

Orlin followed the Professor into the cabin. The cooing of a happy pigeon greeted him as he entered the room. Bernice began to shudder as Orlin approached. The professor stared at the bird.

"They do that when they're excited," explained Orlin.

"I made her comfortable, Mr. Orlin. I put this fine mesh over the box to keep her from messing the cabin. I think she's recovered from what ailed her."

Orlin reached in and picked up Bernice. He held her up and the bird slapped his face with her wings. He examined her eyes and found them clear. "She's fine, Professor. You know, she's special. I picked her out of a hundred birds at the show. She's my lady."

"Well, I'm glad I found her," said Tyrell. "I know you're fond of your ladies. Now you sit down here and have a cup of tea and a cookie with me before you start for home."

Orlin sat by the fire with Bernice on his lap. The Professor talked about other rescues he'd made in the woods. After his tea, Orlin stood to leave. "Thanks. Professor You saved Bernice from coyotes, finding her the way you did."

"Well, I'm glad I stumbled upon her. Now, how are you going to get her home?"

"That's easy," said Orlin. He stepped through the door and pointed Bernice toward the dovecote in Turner's Grove. Lifting his arms in the air, he let Bernice fly. She rose toward the clouds in the direction of Mrs. Story's boarding house.

"I guess that's why they call them homing pigeons," said the Professor.

"She'll be there when I get back. She's my lady. Thanks, Professor."

Tyrell waved goodbye and watched Orlin start through the trees.

On Monday morning Orlin Fingerpott almost skipped to the Broken Star Café for his coffee break. He climbed onto the stool near the cash register to watch Doris work the counter.

"Did Bernice return?" asked Doris.

Orlin gave her a big grin and told her how the Professor had found Bernice near Turner Lake. He glanced toward the swinging door. Rick poked his head through the kitchen window.

"There's a lot of weather out today, Orlin."

"Yes, Mr. Moon, there is." Orlin paused, "Is your niece working today?"

Rick winked at Doris. "No, she's flown the coop and gone back to Minneapolis. You know how ladies are, they come and go." Rick laughed.

"Just like Bernice," said Orlin.

"Just like beautiful ladies," said Rick.

Outside the cafe Orlin searched the sky for an airplane. He lifted his cap and scratched his head. The sky opened to him like an empty hand.

Faces From a Broken Star

CHAPTER SIX

Gilbert's Dilemma

As a boy Gilbert Temple came to the Broken Star Café on Saturdays after baseball practice. He'd climb onto a stool, lay his glove with the baseball in the pocket on the counter, and order a chocolate milkshake.

After graduation from high school, Gilbert managed to finish two years at Presser Community College and played for the junior varsity team. He still lived in Turner's Grove and frequented the Broken Star on Saturdays. It was there that he told Doris and Rick about the call he had received from Chicago.

It wasn't a call from a semi-pro team, but from the A.G. Spalding Sporting Goods Company in Chicago. He was to work in the manufacture of baseballs. If he couldn't play professional ball at least he would become part of the national pastime.

Three years went by and Gilbert sat on a stool similar to the one at the Broken Star. This one was in Chicago where he pulled eighty-eight inches of red thread through the leather hide of a baseball. He counted two, four, six, eight and registered one hundred stitches to go. He rotated the leather on the vise and pulled the cover around the inside core. With luck he'd finish twenty-eight baseballs in a day.

Gilbert began thinking about how many baseballs he'd sewn in three years? His fingers worked deftly, a needle in each hand. One hundred and forty balls a week for fifty weeks. Seven thousand balls a year. That's twenty-one thousand baseballs in three years. He glanced down the row of workers, their fingers flying.

He, alone, had sewed enough baseballs each year to supply all the major league teams for a season. Gilbert cut the thread. "That has to be worth something," he mumbled. He placed the finished ball on the tray and thought of his friends. How tiresome their jokes had become. "How does it feel, Gilbert, when Griffey hits one of your balls over the fence?"

Gilbert, a proud man, was happy to play even a small part in the national pastime. Spalding had revolutionized baseball by the manufacture of sports equipment. But Gilbert found it hard to explain his work so that others would take it seriously. To Gilbert a baseball remained a marvel of construction. How many people knew that a baseball had a cork interior called a 'pill,' and was wrapped precisely in cowhide taken only from Holstein cattle? He could feel pride in that. Gilbert thought a baseball's dimensions must be as interesting to others as it was to him.

"Did you say something, Gilbert?" asked Rita from the next stool.

"Not really," he said, pulling thread through the leather.

Gilbert's thoughts turned to Darlene at the library. How could he describe her? He looked at the baseball before him. Perfectly stitched together, that's how. She made him feel like he'd hit the ball out of the park. Maybe it was the way her hair barely touched her shoulders and bounced as she turned her head. Or was it her blue eyes that made him want to dive in and go swimming? But Darlene was that elusive fly ball just over the fielder's head, landing for a triple. He had no chance of catching her.

Gilbert visited the library after work and listened to Darlene talk about authors and music. He imagined sitting across from her at Gino's Italian Restaurant on Fourth Avenue drinking a glass of Chianti. Impossible! But what if it did happen? What if she agreed to go out with him? He constructed the conversation in his mind.

"What do you do, Gilbert?"

"It's kind of hard to explain."

"I'm interested."

Gilbert considered. "I work for the A.G. Spalding sporting goods company."

Darlene would sip her wine and lift her blue eyes.

"I'm in baseballs."

He imagined the long silence. He would be unable to help himself. "A baseball weighs between five and five and quarter ounces and measures between nine and nine-and-a-quarter inches in circumference. It has a cork center and is surrounded by wrappings of wool and polyester/cotton yarn, and is covered by stitched cowhide."

Gilbert could picture it clearly. Darlene, lowering her eyes as a plate of lasagna was set before her. He would talk on and on and on. "A baseball has a cowhide cover. It must be white and stitched together with waxed red thread 88 inches long. The cowhide is tested for seventeen potential deficiencies before it is approved for use in Major League baseball. It takes exactly one hundred and eight stitches in the sewing process and every ball is sewed by hand."

Gilbert's fingers worked the thread: two, four, six; two, four, six. The scene at Gino's would not go away. He saw himself take a deep breath as Darlene nibbled her lasagna.

"Gilbert, what exactly do you do at Spalding?"

He would twirl his spaghetti. Here was a lovely dream sitting across from him. "I'm vice- president of production," he wanted to say. Instead he said, "I'm a stitcher."

"Interesting." Darlene nodded and took a sip of wine.

"I average between four and five baseballs an hour. That's 7,000 of my balls a year that go to Major League teams."

Fool! He'd brace himself for a rejoinder. But Darlene wasn't the vulgar male you find at Shauney's' Tavern. God, men were repulsive.

Gilbert looked over at Rita. He felt his face grow hot. He imagined how boring this conversation would sound to anyone with an ounce of brain.

Darlene would never go out with him. Even if she did, he'd strike out and there was nothing he could do about it.

He saw it all now as he placed another baseball on the tray. Darlene would lift her glass.

"Here's to baseball," she'd say.

"Strike three," the umpire would yell. Like a fly ball, Gilbert would lose her in the lights.

After work Gilbert met Ed at Shauney's. "I'm a total ass," he said. "What am I to do?"

Ed appraised Gilbert over his beer, "About being an ass you mean?"

Gilbert stared at him.

"Do you really want my advice?"

Gilbert nodded.

"Don't talk about your balls all the time."

"I don't know anything else," said Gilbert.

"If she goes out with you, which according to you is as likely as the two of us being signed by the Yankees, ask her about herself. Talk to her, 'What do you like to do when you're not at the library?' 'Tell me about your family.'"

"I'm no good at small talk," said Gilbert.

"That's my advice," said Ed.

Gilbert shrugged and finished his beer.

He strolled to the library and waited at the counter. Gilbert watched Darlene scan books with complete efficiency. An elderly lady moved away. His heart sounded like a jack-hammer.

Darlene turned to him, "Can I help you?"

"I feel like such a dolt," he managed. "Nietzsche, I'm looking for one of his books."

"You'll probably find it in the Philosophy section."

"I've looked and couldn't find the one I want."

Darlene tapped a few keys on the computer. "What's the title?"

"Thus spoke something," Gilbert stammered.

"*Thus Spoke Zarathustra*," she smiled.

"That's it."

She wrote the call number on a slip of paper. Gilbert found the book and carried it to a table. He read for an hour and put Nietzsche on the shelf. The next night he recovered the book and read:

> *O man, take care!*
> *What does the deep midnight declare?*
> *I was asleep —*
> *From a deep dream I woke and swear:*

Gilbert raised his eyes from the book to find Darlene standing beside the table. "Are you really interested in Nietzsche?" she asked.

Gilbert blinked.

"Somehow, you don't look like a Nietzsche fan."

He pushed the book aside. "I went to a baseball game last week," he said. "The man next to me was reading this book before the game. He seemed oblivious to everything around him. There I sat caught up in the sights and sounds of the stadium and he was reading."

"He was reading Nietzsche at a baseball game?" Darlene laughed.

"I decided it must be a good book if he brought it to the ballpark."

"Well, I've read it," said Darlene. "But I wouldn't take it to a baseball game."

"You wouldn't?"

"No, I love baseball too much," she said.

"You do?"

Gilbert gazed into Darlene's blue eyes. He thought he heard the solid crack of the ball hitting the bat. He imagined a fly ball sailing toward him in center field. He saw himself tracking it perfectly, ready for a spectacular catch. Gilbert pulled two tickets to a Cub's game from his pocket and laid them on the table.

Darlene picked them up.

"I work for the A.G. Spaulding Sporting Goods Company," said Gilbert. "Would you like to go to a game this Saturday?"

Darlene smiled. "I'd love to," she said. "But only if you leave Nietzsche behind."

CHAPTER SEVEN

The Dish Ran Away With the Spoon

This story begins with the last line of a nursery rhyme: *the dish ran away with the spoon.* In the end you may think it all 'hey-diddle-diddle,' foolishness; but for Henry Taylor it led him to marriage and two adored children.

Henry owned a farm between Turner's Grove and Presser on Painter's Brush Road.

He and Florence settled into life on the farm following their honeymoon at the Rose Marie Bed and Breakfast in Lincoln. They were both frugal people. Their only extravagance that first year was dinner at the Broken Star Café on the fourth Friday of each month.

Henry was short and wide, the round dish in our nursery rhyme. Florence, on the other hand, reminded anyone who noticed her of a spoon: tall and thin on top, but wider at the bottom.

Henry stood five feet, four inches tall. His short arms seemed to belong to someone else. Henry waddled rather than walked and friends called him penguin. But Henry didn't mind. He was always too jovial and happy for that to matter. As the spoon in the story, Florence had long arms and gave the impression that she could tie her shoes without bending over. Seeing Henry and Florence seated together at the Broken Star made quite a table setting.

On any fourth Friday they ate at the same table. Henry sat with his chin a few inches above the tabletop. Florence bent over her soup bowl so as not to spill on her night-out dress. They seemed an odd couple; but no matter, they loved each other. Their marriage proved that opposites do attract and nursery rhymes learned early are remembered.

Work on the farm did not discourage romance. From this union came two children. This would be a fairly common story if the resemblance to their parents had not been a factor.

Their first child, Lyle, was born on June 21, the longest day of the year. Henry witnessed the birth. His first thought was that Florence was giving birth to one of those elongated balloons that clowns twist into animal figures. The doctor said the baby's legs were so long he expected to see basketball shoes on the baby's feet. He placed the newborn onto the mother's stomach. Florence blinked and gave a sigh of relief.

It was no surprise to Florence that the second child should be short like Henry. They named her Sable. It wasn't long before she was nicknamed 'Stub.' Sable grew up hating all things round and short like beach balls and oval night stands. No matter, Sable was adored by her father. Florence thought this was because they could talk on the same level.

In the meantime, Florence doted on her tall son. Of course, the parents loved both children; but there was something in their natures that drew Henry to Sable and Florence to Lyle.

Now we come to a tricky part of our story. You might recall the Good Book's admonition: the sins of the parents are visited upon their children from generation to generation. Henry and Florence did not think of their statures as sinful, and Lyle and Sable didn't hold their parents responsible for the odd gene pool. But as they became adults, Lyle and Sable began to wonder.

"Why didn't I get mother's slender figure?" complained Sable.

"Why didn't I get father's…," but Lyle stopped there. He really did not want to be as short as his father. He simply didn't want to be asked again and again if he played basketball.

"There's nothing for it," said Sable. "We are who we are. *Hey diddle, diddle, the cat and the fiddle, the cow jumped over the moon. The little dog laughed to see such a sport…*"

"… *and the dish ran away with the spoon*," finished Lyle. "We have to make a pact, the two of us."

"What sort of pact?"

"We must never marry and pass our genes on to another generation."

Sable frowned at this. She doubted that anyone would want to marry someone who looked like they came out of a pinball machine. "Maybe you're right," she said.

But Sable had not counted on Albert, the 'miniature pony man' at the Lincoln Park Zoo. Albert was not tall and handsome, but he loved shortness in horses. He did not find it much of a leap to love shortness in people. Sable watched Albert give pony rides to the children and was warmed by his gentle ways.

Albert reminded Sable that if he had been tall he would have worked with thoroughbreds and they would never have met. It seemed the perfect match and they were married.

Lyle fell in love on a warm October afternoon. It was his habit to drive to a farm on the north side of town and walk through the corn-maze. All Heart Farm was owned by a tall, slender woman the children called the Corn-Maze-Lady. Her real name was Fiona Post.

Lyle and Fiona noticed each other at once because they were the only heads that rose above the corn stalks. Their eyes met and they followed each other to the end of a row of sweet corn. While children pushed away the stalks trying to find a way out of the maze, Fiona handed Lyle an ear of corn. She didn't know why she did this, but Lyle took it in his hands and gently peeled away the husk. Fiona broke out in a sweat and unconsciously checked her clothing. And so the seed was planted for another perfect union.

It is true that the two romances confused everyone who knew them. It meant a change of table setting. You no longer had a dish running away with a spoon, but a spoon running away with a spoon, and a dish running away with a dish. The earth seemed to be turning in the direction of normality.

Rick and Doris at the Broken Star Café took notice. Before the children, Albert had sat at one end of the table and Florence at the other. This arrangement seemed to tilt the table downhill toward Albert. When Lyle and Sable with their spouses joined Albert and Florence for dinner, their mother made sure the seating was dish spoon, dish spoon, dish spoon. Surprisingly, the table seemed to level itself.

This, of course, is not the entire story. We haven't mentioned the little dog, Snort, and the cow, Moonlight. How silly it would be to include them in this otherwise believable fairy tale.

CHAPTER EIGHT

A Figment of the Imagination

Charlie Little parked his pickup between the diagonal lines in front of the Broken Star Café. It was seven o'clock a.m. He hopped up on the usual stool at the counter. Not much of a talker, Charlie sat between Bill Garland and Terry Morgan listening to their complaints and banter. "Charlie, is your wheat ready?" Charlie nodded, but his mind was elsewhere.

For twenty years Charlie had imagined he owned a bookstore. When asked about this, Charlie explained, "It's a dream I have. It began while driving my Chalmers combine twenty years ago."

Like his father and grandfather, Charlie raised winter wheat in southern Nebraska. He'd go on to say, "Wheat is in my soul, but books are in my heart." Charlie loved to watch the wheat fields turn gold at harvest time, but after work he enjoyed reading.

On a good day, Charlie measured five feet, five inches tall. He called this a height impediment. His small stature, along with his quiet ways, often caused Charlie to be overlooked. He didn't mind. He preferred to be alone. At family gatherings someone would say, "Has anyone seen Charlie?" Heads would shake and someone else would laugh and yell, "Who's Charlie?"

"Arlene, go find your brother," demanded her mother. "He'll be in his room."

His sister would find Charlie folded into his favorite overstuffed chair next to his bedroom window. He believed no one could see him behind a book.

Charlie never left the farm. Arlene married Sam Stanwood and Charlie stayed on to help his parents. When they died in 1972 within months of one another, Charlie continued to work the farm. In his spare time he visited used bookstores and filled the vacant rooms with more shelves.

Charlie turned forty-five in 1987 and began thinking seriously of buying a bookstore. His thoughts turned into a dream late one August evening. It happened like this. Dust blew thick over the wheat field Charlie was cutting. As it grew darker he turned on the combine's lights to extend the day's work. The weather had cooled slightly. He'd been driving the Chalmers for twelve hours. He blinked and stared ahead through the wind shield. At the end of the field he thought he saw a building.

Charlie stopped the combine and wiped the sweat from his eyes. He got out of the cab and walked a few feet up the row silhouetted by the headlights. It was the darndest thing. The building wasn't there. He climbed back into the cab and made another loop around the field. When he approached the same place he saw the building again. He could even describe it in detail. It was one story, bricked in front, with a large display window to the side of the center door. Charlie rubbed his eyes. Across the building stretched a sign in blue letters: *Charlie Little Books*.

The rest of that night Charlie imagined working in his bookstore. While the combine continued to pour wheat into trucks, Charlie disappeared. His hands drove the machine, but his heart worked in the bookstore. In Charlie's mind a building had sprouted like rich wheat at the end of his field.

With each turn around the field Charlie looked through the

combine's windshield. He could almost see himself unlock the door and place the open sign in the window. He saw himself step to the back room and switch on the lights. Charlie straightened the counter by the front door and put money in the cash register. He dusted the shelves and grabbed a broom to swept the sidewalk in front of the shop.

The next morning Charlie returned to The Broken Star. Turner's Grove was thriving at this time with wheat farms. Rick's place drew farmers together like pigs to the trough. Fields were too wet for cutting at 6:00 a. m., and farmers waited over a hot cups of coffee. Doris poured coffee for Charlie. "I'm going to open a bookstore," he mumbled.

Doris stared at Charlie and pulled at her ear. "What's that, Charlie?"

"I'm going to open a bookstore," repeated Charlie.

"When will this be?" asked Doris.

Charlie lifted his cup, "I'll let you know."

Bill Garland sat next to Charlie. "Your house is a bookstore," he said.

"That may be," said Charlie, sipping the last of his coffee. "But this is different. Well, best get at it, the wheat doesn't harvest itself." He dropped a tip on the counter and disappeared.

At noon the field crew stopped for lunch. They took their places in the shade of the combine. Charlie's neighbor, Terry Morgan, sat against the tire and uncorked his thermos, "What do you think, Charlie?"

"Well," he scratched his head. "I'd like to sell books."

"You're always talking about books."

"I'm going to open a bookstore."

"You ain't got a bookstore."

Charlie didn't answer. He knew he was being humored. Many in Turner's Grove thought he was joking and simply went along with him.

"How are book sales?" asked Doris.

"I have a nice set of Dickens," said Charlie. "Are you interested?"

"Not much time for reading I'm afraid," said Doris.

"You might want it as a gift for someone. You let me know," said Charlie.

"I'll think about it," said Doris.

Charlie continued to dream. It didn't matter if he was harvesting wheat, repairing a fence, or feeding stock. Charlie could turn the key of his imagination and place an Open sign in the window. In his mind he arranged new stock that customers brought to trade or sell. Sometimes Charlie would be missing from The Broken Star for days.

"Has anyone seen Charlie?" asked Doris.

The regulars at the counter laughed. Rick poked his head from the kitchen window. "He's somewhere talking books." Everyone nodded and sipped their coffee. His neighbors agreed Charlie must be referring to the books in his house. Newcomers in town assumed from their conversation that Charlie owned a bookstore in another town.

In 2007 Charlie turned sixty-five and was getting too old to care for a large farm. He leased out his fields and hired Lyle Townsend to help with the stock. It was about this time Charlie noticed the obituary in the newspaper.

> *Henry Larson, owner of Barrow's Gift Shop,*
> *died yesterday at the age of eighty-seven.*

Henry's shop was directly across from the Broken Star Café. Charlie began watching for sale notices in the *Turner Reporter*. The next week he saw an announcement that the merchandise from the gift shop had been sold to Myrtle's Boutique in Lincoln. But the building was up for sale. Charlie drove to the Turner Bank.

"What about Henry Larson's store?" he asked Ben Sacks, the bank manager.

"Well, it's for sale. His kids don't want it. They live in St. Louis and aren't interested in a small town like ours."

"I'm interested," said Charlie.

Ben Sacks fixed a puzzled eye on Charlie. "Charlie, you're sixty-five years old. Most men your age sell out and buy a place in Florida. They certainly don't go into business."

Charlie stared at the floor. He raised his head and pulled at his chin. "Ben, I've owned this bookstore in my mind for twenty years.

Now I want to open it. I've saved the money."

Ben Sacks laughed. He nodded his head. "I'll look into it."

"I've saved all my life," said Charlie. "I'd like to do what I've always wanted to do before I die." Charlie put on his cap with the Chalmers insignia and got up to leave.

Ben Sacks rose from his desk. "Stop in tomorrow. I'll have an answer."

By mid-March Charlie was fingering the key in his pocket. For twenty years he'd imagined this day. He stood before the door and placed the key in the lock.

Charlie Little opened the door and stepped over the threshold. The building needed work and Charlie began clearing out what he didn't need. He spent the next several weeks painting the walls and arranging for carpet to be installed. He asked the Shaw brothers to build a counter and bookshelves for the outside walls.

Charlie drove to Lincoln and dropped off his idea for a shop sign: 'Charlie Little Books'.

Below, in smaller print, were the words: 'Charlie Little, Bookseller'. He ordered a smaller sign that read: 'We buy books in good condition.' He paid for a third placard to be placed in the store's window on opening day.

Charlie hired Glen Johnson to brick the front of the building so others could see what he'd seen from his combine. By May he was moving books from his house onto the shelves. Charlie put an ad in the Turner Reporter:

Charlie Little announces the grand opening
of Charlie Little Books.
An open house will be held from 5:00 to 9:00 p.m. Monday, June 1st.
Refreshments will be served.

His next visit was to the Broken Star Café.

"Haven't seen much of you," said Doris.

"I've been sort of busy."

"So I hear. The big day's coming."

Charlie laid a list on the counter. "I'd hoped you'd cater the punch, sandwiches, and finger food. Parker's Bakery is making pastries. Would Rick do that?"

Doris smiled. "I'm sure he would be happy too, Charlie."

"Let me know the cost and I'll write you a check." Charlie tipped his cap and ambled out the door.

Monday morning, June 1st, Charlie unlocked the door of his shop. He hung the Open sign in the window and switched on the lights. He dusted the counter and put money in the till. Charlie grabbed a broom to sweep the sidewalk just as he'd done in his imagination.

A few customers came in during the day to congratulate him. Turner Bank sent flowers to honor the occasion. Doris arrived at three o'clock. She placed paper cups on a table just inside the door.

"The sandwiches and snacks will be here before five," she said.

Charlie nodded. He'd purchased four easy-chairs and two glass-fronted bookcases from Yesterday's Memory Antique Mall in Lincoln. These made a sitting area in the center of the store. Charlie pointed to the arrangement. "We'll put the food there," he said. Doris smiled and returned to the cafe.

Charlie reached behind the counter and found the placard from the printers. He set it in the front of the window.

Charlie Little Books
Imagined, August 1987
Opened, June 1, 2007

At 5:00 residents of Turner's Grove poured into the small shop. Townspeople filled the isles. Punch was poured and food sampled. The hours went by. Out of the hubbub someone shouted, "Has anyone seen Charlie?"

The room grew quiet. Bill Garland called out, "Arlene, will you go find your brother?"

Everyone laughed. Charlie poked his head from the back room and waved a book at his friends.

Bill Garland raised his glass, "Here's to Charlie Little, Bookseller, and the most patient man I ever met."

Faces From a Broken Star

CHAPTER NINE

The Professor

One windy day in September a stranger walked into the Broken Star Café. Doris poured coffee. The man smiled. "I walked through the cemetery at the end of town," he said. "There was a grave with the name, The Professor. Around the grave were small stones set in cement."

Doris set the coffee pot on the counter and smiled. "Do you have a while?"

"I guess so."

"The grave belongs to Tyrell Williams, the only black man in Turner's Grove. He had a cabin on Turner Lake. No one knows exactly how long he lived there or where he came from. He was a regular and sat at that booth every Tuesday." Doris pointed across the aisle. She reached under the counter and placed a booklet before the stranger. "We have a local writer in town who has gathered some information about The Professor and published this story. You can read it here if you like or buy a copy at the bookstore across the street."

The stranger moved to the Professor's booth and opened the booklet:

Tyrell Williams was a tall, gaunt man. I often thought of him as a black Henry David Thoreau walking the woods. People in Turner's Grove called him The Professor. This story is gathered from the people who knew him. It begins at the Broken Star Café. Here's how I remember The professor...

"Doris, don't forget the reserved sign on table three," said Rick.

"I remember. It's Tuesday. The Professor will walk in from Turner Lake."

"Remember the time he found someone sat in his booth," asked Rick. He turned right around and walked out. He didn't make a fuss or complain. He just left without a word."

"I remember," said Doris. "I've reserved his booth ever since."

Tyrell Williams slipped on his slouch hat and wound a rope around the latch on the cabin door to keep it from blowing open. He wrapped a book in a plastic sack and carried his shoes through the trees to Town Road. Tyrell took care to walk on the verge of the highway, feeling the earth under his feet. He paused to listen to the rustle of a small animal in the brushes and stooped to pick up a flat rock.

In forty minutes he arrived at Will's Farm Supply and put on his shoes. He walked along the street and looked in the window of Charlie Little's Bookstore. He'd stop in after breakfast. The bell over the café door rang as he entered the Broken Star. Tyrell lifted his eyes to the booth in the corner and found it empty. He sat down, opened the plastic bag, and pulled out his book, *The Life of Olaudah Equiano*.

"Here's your coffee, Professor?" said Doris.

Tyrell raised his eyes from his book and smiled. "It's a pleasure to see you this morning, Ms. Doris. And yes, coffee and a good book in a nice place, that's fine."

Doris smiled and poured coffee into a Broken Star mug. "What are you reading today, Professor?"

"I've always got something, you know. It doesn't seem right to sit down and not have something to read. You've never been to my cabin, have you?"

"No, I haven't."

"Well you come and visit some time. It will surprise you, I think."

"Will you have something to eat, Professor?"

"I'd like oatmeal and two slices of wheat toast if Mr. Rick is cooking, thank you."

"You enjoy your book, Professor. Breakfast won't take long."

Tyrell bent his head to his book and shut out the voices of farmers and regulars at the other tables. In a few minutes Doris returned oatmeal and toast. "You never did tell me what you're reading."

"No, I guess I didn't." Tyrell glanced at his book and then at Doris. "I'm afraid it's nothing popular like most people read. It's a book I just happened on, *The Life of Olaudah Equiano*. He was a slave in the eighteenth century."

"I'm sure it's beyond me," said Doris.

"Now, Ms. Doris, you shouldn't say that. You belittle yourself. We all have the gift of intelligence. Don't let anyone tell you differently."

"Well, I don't read much. When I do it's usually a good mystery."

"A good mystery is just fine," said Tyrell.

Doris topped off his coffee cup and moved to the next table. Tyrell returned to his book. Conversations filled the room and Tyrell read until Doris brought his check and offered to refill on his coffee.

"Thank you, Ms. Doris. But I'd better go." He reached in his pocket and pulled out two flat rocks. He pointed to the plain one. I found this stone this morning and will have to work on it a bit. But this one is finished. I painted a Scarab on it as symbol of the rising sun and new life. It's for you."

Doris held the painted rock in her hand and marveled at the delicacy of the colors.

"I haven't given you a Scarab before, have I?" asked Tyrell.

"No Professor. It's beautiful. Thank you. You do beautiful work. You shouldn't just give them away. You should sell these."

"Oh no, Ms. Doris, I find pleasure in giving them. You put it in your room to remind yourself that every day is a new creation. Tyrell picked up his check and slipped his book in the plastic bag. He paid at the cash register, pulled on his hat, and left the Broken Star.

Doris dropped the scarab rock in her pocket and returned to the counter. She watched out the window as Tyrell crossed the street and entered Charlie Little's bookstore.

"Good morning Professor," said Charlie. "I'm just straitening up in here. How can I help you?"

"I'm going to browse a bit," said Tyrell. He drifted to the back of the bookstore. He found Charlie's shelves pleasantly arranged. The books were in good condition and he knew where to find what he wanted. Tyrell spent half an hour scanning the shelves before returning to the counter."

"What did you find, Professor?" asked Charlie.

Tyrrell placed a small copy of *Winesburg Ohio* on the counter.

"A good choice," said Charlie. "But then I've never known you to make a bad choice."

"Mr. Charlie, it's too late in life and I have no time for bad reading. If a book doesn't suit me in the first few pages, I put it aside."

"I understand." Charlie raised his eyes to the Professor. "Don't you get lonely out there by the lake? I thought you might like to move to Jude's Mobile Home Park and be closer to town."

"No, Mr. Charlie, I'm just fine in my cabin. You should come for a visit."

Charlie gave Tyrell his change. "You know I'd like that."

"You'd be welcome." Tyrell reached into his pocket and pulled out a flat rock with a book painted in bright colors. "This is for you, Mr. Charlie. It's a symbol of wisdom."

Tyrell slipped the new book in his sack and left the shop. He stopped briefly at Ma's Grocery and started for home. At the edge of town he pulled off his shoes and socks to walk in the grass. As he neared his cabin he saw a park ranger's car pulled to the side of the road. The ranger was bending over something. Tyrell stopped abruptly as a gunshot echoed through the woods. He approached the scene and saw the deer lying in the ditch.

The ranger looked up, "Hit by a car. I had to put him down."

Tyrell bent and stroked the deer's soft fur.

"The bastard didn't even stop," said the Ranger.

Tyrell wiped the tears from his eyes. "It's a shame," he said. "She's one of nature's beautiful paintings."

A few days later Charlie Little knocked on the Professor's door. "Come in Mr. Charlie and sit by the fire. I'm glad you've come. I'll make us some tea." Charlie glanced over the room.

The cabin reminded him of his old farm house. Books lined every wall. The two chairs by the fireplace were old. A kerosene lamp sat on each side table. The cabin had been carefully chinked on the outside and was warm inside. A welcoming glow from the fireplace spread over the floor.

The Professor brought a tray from a small corner kitchen. "I usually eat near the fire," he said. Tyrell set the tray on a large desk spread with papers and books.

"Here you go Mr. Charlie. Its good and hot and a tasty cookie from Ma's Grocery."

"Thank you Professor. I must say, you have a nice place here. I can understand why you don't want to leave."

"It suits me, Mr. Charlie." Tyrell laughed. "It wasn't so when I moved in. I had to evict the local residents. The crows and mice and spiders didn't like that one bit. I was younger then and did most of the work myself."

Charlie took a sip of tea. "I didn't know you had so many books."

"Few people visit, so I guess word doesn't get out. It's just as well. I like my quiet. It allows me to read and paint my rock pictures." Tyrell pointed to a small table under a window. "I paint when I get tired of reading. If the weather's nice I walk in the woods or sit by the lake. On Tuesday I treat myself to breakfast at the Star and visit you at the bookstore."

"A fine way to live," said Charlie. You must have as many books on your shelves as I do in the store."

"Well, I wouldn't guess so, but I just can't part with them you know."

"I understand. My home was much like this before I opened the shop. You have family, Professor?"

"No, Mr. Charlie, they're all gone. I'm alone. But, you know, I'm a happy man. I don't have a real education. I guess I'm what you call self-taught. But I have everything I need. I bought this cabin with my savings from hard work. And I live on a small pension, but it's a good life."

Charlie looked long at the professor. "Don't you ever want to travel or visit the city?"

"Oh, I've traveled some and I've lived in the city. In the city I see people scurrying about hustle and bustle. Here I am, no telephone, no radio, no television, and I'm just fine. I have woods to walk in, sunsets to watch, and a fire to keep me warm. And most of all I have my books." Tyrell paused a moment.

"I remember someone saying, 'I read to know that I'm not alone,'" said Charlie.

"A great truth," agreed Tyrell.

"Well, you're unique among men Professor. I must get back to the store. Somehow, I think we're kindred spirits."

Tyrell led him to the door and handed Charlie a small rock with a painted turtle. "This is the sign of endurance and patience, Mr. Charlie. And you are such a man."

Charlie put the stone in his pocket. When he returned to his shop, he placed the turtle in the flower pot with others Tyrell had given him and smiled.

In the Café the stranger raised his head from the story as Doris filled his cup. He thanked her and read on.

The story of The Professor's life is not long or complicated. His is the story of a man who is at home in his own skin. The Professor never talked about peace, but when you were with him you felt peaceful. He never told another person how to live or what to believe. But when you talked with him, you felt valued by something greater than yourself. The Professor's kindness was always perfectly timed, as illustrated in this next incident.

The Professor always stopped by Ma's Grocery on his way home to pick up a few things. He was there one day when Beverly Wilson and her five-year-old son, Peter were shopping for groceries. Tyrell picked a loaf of bread from a shelf on aisle three. Peter and his mother came toward him. Peter, never shy, pointed at Tyrell and said in a loud voice, "Look Mommy, he's black like my black crayon." Beverly immediately clapped her hand over Peter's mouth and said, "Shush, it's not nice to point."

Tyrell smiled and continued around the corner to next aisle. Peter walked toward him again with his finger raised high. He passed Tyrell and shouted in a loud voice, "You're like my black crayon." Beverly pulled Peter away and mumbled, "Sorry, Professor."

Tyrell, pushed his grocery cart to the check-out counter. He turned when he felt something poke him in the leg. Peter stared up at him and asked, "Why are you black Mr.?"

Tyrell turned to Beverly with a smile and said, "May I explain?" Red-faced, she nodded. By this time everyone was listening. Tyrell got down on one knee. He pulled a rock out of his pocket. Why he had this particular rock on that day no one knew. He showed the rock to Peter.

"Look at this Mr. Peter. On this side is a white swan like you." Tyrell turned the rock over. "On this side is a black swan like me. The One who makes all swans likes to color some white, some black, and some other colors. They're all beautiful, just like the colors in your crayon box. This rock is for you, a gift from a black swan to a white swan."

No one spoke. The checkout line stood still. Then someone applauded and everyone began talking at once. "Thank you, Professor," said Beverly. Peter smiled and turned the rock over in his hand before putting it in his pocket.

In late October when the leaves were bright, a patrol car drove toward Turner's Grove. The officer first spotted the book, its pages fluttering in the wind and then the shoes on the road. The Professor's body lay at almost the same spot where the deer had fallen. A car had come over the hill and hit Tyrell, throwing him into a ditch. In his cabin they found a will leaving his books to Charlie Little. But this was not the end of The Professor's story.

The Professor's life had melted into the life of the town. Everyone in Turners Grove had received a gift from the Professor. The funeral took place on a Tuesday morning. All the shops closed for the service. Everyone gathered in the cemetery. Each carried at least one stone, and some, many stones received from Tyrell. If you go to his grave today you will find the scarab, the turtle, the book, and the black and white swan around the Professor's grave.

Doris noticed the man close the booklet and motion to her. When she approached the stranger said, "Thank you. It's a wonderful story. I'll buy a copy at the bookstore. The Professor sounds like a wonderful person."

"He was," she said. Doris reached in a basket on the counter and handed the stranger a flat stone with a black swan painted on the surface. "Take this with you," said Doris. "And come back again."

CHAPTER TEN

Swimming with Victor

Gerald Adam stretched a little further for the last apple. Why not? At seventy his wiry body had served him well. Hell, he still power-walked the perimeter of the mobile home park five days a week, mowed his own lawn, and bowled with a forty-pound ball.

As he reached for the last apple the ladder tipped and Gerald's eyes registered disbelief. Like the first Adam, the illusive fruit undid Gerald. A day later he woke up at Pane Municipal Hospital wearing a new hip.

"We're going to turn you now, Mr. Adam," said Nurse Braun. Gerald noticed her sumo-broad arms and didn't argue.

"You're not the first Adam to fall for an apple," she snorted.

Fuzzy from the morphine, Gerald thought of Sir Isaac Newton. But it was his wife's voice he heard out of the fog. "Didn't I tell him he was too old to be climbing ladders? He wouldn't listen. That's a stubborn knot between his ears."

That was a month ago. He vaguely remembered waking up from recovery, grumbling through daily, rehab and hearing the doctor say, "You still have work to do."

"What do you mean, doc?"

"You need to strengthen that hip. I suggest staying off ladders and putting away the Viagra for the time being." The doctor smiled. "I want you to continue in the Presser pool."

"Water rehab!"

"That's right. Three times a week. Your wife can drive you. It's either swim laps or take water-aerobics."

The following Wednesday Gerald sat in the pool dressing room. He watched the crooked and bent old men struggle to pull on their swim suits. God, he grimaced, what a skin and bone shop. The frayed heads of hair and pale bodies reminded Gerald of a field of dried corn stalks after harvest. He glanced down at his own legs. "Damn apples," he said out loud.

Gerald edged himself into lane three at the shallow end of the pool. He swam to the halfway point and saw a large bubble pass him on the right. At first he thought someone had thrown a beach ball into the pool. His eye registered a round object with side paddles turning at high speed. At the end of the pool a chubby body with flippers on his feet waited for Gerald.

"Hi, my name is Victor," said a shrill voice in lane two. "Old people are supposed to use lanes five and six."

Gerald wiped the water from his eyes and stared down at a child the height of Donald Duck. Victor pointed at the sign on the wall. REHAB: LANES FIVE AND SIX. "It's okay. I won't tell. I'm only here because I'm fat."

Gerald looked over his shoulder. Victor continued talking. "My doctor told my mom that if I didn't lose weight, I'd have to be hauled to the school bus in a back-hoe by the time I was ten."

"How old are you?" asked Gerald.

"I'm seven and a half. But I'm a lot older in pounds. I have to exercise and give up stuff." Gerald pushed off the wall for the return lap. As he neared the other end he was passed again by Victor the bubble.

"You swim good," said Victor.

Gerald frowned.

"Maybe we could swim together on Wednesdays."

"Look, Victor. I'm not your grandfather."

"My grandfather's dead," said Victor. "That's my mom on the bench reading the Bible."

Gerald noticed a large woman lift her eyes from her book and tattoo a message on his forehead: "I'm watching you with my darling boy."

Pushing off from the wall, Gerald began another lap. He'd swim faster this time. He was almost to the other end when Victor raced by.

"How do you do it, kid? How do you swim so fast?"

"My mom says I have a gift. My dad says I have an energizer battery up my you-know what." Victor grabbed his behind. "Do you know what my name means?"

Gerald stared down the lane.

"It means conqueror. My mom looked it up in a baby book. If I was a girl my name would be Vicki and I wouldn't have a …" Victor pointed to the front of his swim suit.

Gerald wiped the sweat from his forehead. "Well Victor, I have to leave now." Gerald climbed carefully out of the pool and headed for the dressing room.

"Hey, wait for me. I'm done with my exercise today."

Gerald dressed and found Martha in the waiting room. She recognized the scowling face at once. "Is your hip bothering you?"

"I need a of beer," he said and headed for the door. "I've decided to change my workout days to Tuesday, Thursday, and Saturday."

"Why is that?" asked Martha.

"Because I don't want to do rehab with a six and half-year-old beach ball that weights one hundred and twenty pounds and bounces along the surface of the water."

Before the next drive to Presser Martha decided to take a break from Gerald and have breakfast at the Broken Star Café. Doris approached with the coffee pot. "It's unusual seeing you this early."

Martha frowned. "I had to get out of the house. Gerald is driving me fruit-cakes and I don't even like fruit-cake."

"How's he getting along?" asked Doris.

"Oh, alright I guess. He's still using the walker and swimming laps at the pool." Martha paused and sipped her coffee. "You know, I don't think he likes kids much. And it's strange. He keeps muttering things around the house, like 'an apple a day keeps the doctor away, my ass,' things like that."

Gerald arrived on Thursday and spotted the rehab sign. He lowered himself into lane five and felt the water enfold him. On the ninth lap he lifted his head to see Victor roll by in lane four. Gerald pushed off the far end without stopping. He arrived to find Victor waiting.

"Hi, mister, I guess you're surprised to see me."

Before Gerald let fly the black words forming in his mouth, Victor's mother shifted her weight on the bench and glared in his direction.

"I changed my day because my mom has Women Aglow on Wednesday."

"Don't you go to school?" asked Gerald.

"I'm home-schooled, but I can't read right now because books aren't exercise."

Gerald nodded and pushed off, swimming to the far end. He heard the voice again.

"I can't watch television or play computer games until I lose weight. My mom says she can't afford a forklift."

"Look, Victor the Conqueror, I have work to do. I don't want to be rude, but ..."

"My mom said that Jesus could turn this pool into wine if he wanted to."

"God almighty!" Gerald shouted. His hands accidentally hit the water and sprayed water over Victor. Victor took a step backward and watched his mother bolt toward the pool.

"Get out of there this minute," she yelled.

"Sorry mam. I didn't mean to spray the kid," said Gerald.

Tears filled Victor's eyes. He climbed out of the pool and waddled to the dressing room with his head down. Pinning Gerald with a demo glare Victor's mother marched to the lobby.

Gerald gave Victor time to dress before leaving. He found Martha in the waiting room.

"I just witnessed the oddest thing," she said. "This woman yanked her child by the reception desk and pointed her Bible at the attendant. 'Sin and sorrow,' she screamed. 'God will turn this pool into blood one day.' Then she dragged her son out the door."

Gerald sat in the parking lot and stared through the windshield of the car.

"Is everything alright?" asked Martha

Gerald pointed at the sign on the fence.

>Unauthorized vehicles will be towed.
>JOHN WINESAP TOWING
>332-7448

"I just want out of this nightmare," he said, and Martha started the engine.

Faces From a Broken Star

CHAPTER ELEVEN

May Your Heart Be Glad

Arnold Benson knew right away that he did not like the little man who came through the door of Mayfair Assisted Living. The new facility had been built half way between Pressor and Turner's Grove. Arnold thought the new-comer looked too happy. He sank deeper into his chair and frowned across the foyer. He ran his fingers over his unshaven face and uncombed hair. He bent his head to the buttons on his blue flannel shirt and tapped his right cowboy boot menacingly on the tile floor.

Mrs. Palmer, the Director of Mayfair, approached the new arrival from her office and offered her hand. "You must be Mr. Darlington," she said.

"I am Kingsley Isaac Darlington." He took her hand with a slight bow.

Seeing this, Arnold huffed through his mustache, pushed himself up from his chair and shuffled down the hall toward his room.

Kingsley followed Mrs. Palmer to her office and took a seat before her mahogany desk. "My initials are K.I.D., Mrs. Palmer. I prefer to be called Kid."

Mrs. Palmer lifted her eyes from the folder on her desk and nodded. The information before her described Kingsley as eighty-years-old, five-feet-six-inches tall, one-hundred-and-twenty-five pounds. "You come from Turner's Grove, I see."

Kid balanced his red beret on his knee, revealing a full head of chalk-white hair. He gazed at Mrs. Palmer with sparkling hazel eyes.

"Yes Mam, I lived in Alma Jude's fine mobile home park called the Golden Swan. My Son lives in Presser."

Mrs. Palmer stood and handed Kid the keys to his room. "Welcome to Mayfair," she said.

"Tell me, Mrs. Palmer. Is there transportation to Turner's Grove?"

"Our shuttle runs to Turner's Grove Monday through Friday, Mr. Darlington."

Kid rose from his chair and nodded. "Thank you. May your heart be glad."

Mrs. Palmer, used to, "Have a nice day," smiled as Kid left the office. He walked to room 105 and found his furniture had been delivered according to instructions. File boxes were stacked neatly in the middle of the room labeled: Mysteries, Children's Books, Games & Puzzles, Lego's, Electric Train, and Music Boxes. Kid imagined the movers saying, "Are you sure this is the right address? This is kid's stuff."

Kid laughed at that. If only they knew. He stepped across the living room and pulled back the curtains. Kid looked out on the garden and removed his jacket. As he began to open boxes, there was a quick knock on the door.

"Is everything alright Mr. Darlington?" asked a young lady.

"Everything is fine, please come in?" Kid reached out his hand. "And you are?"

"I'm Angela Sanchez. I clean your room on Tuesdays and Thursdays."

"Thank you, Angela. They call me, Kid. As you can see, my place is not in order, but when it is you are always welcome. And you're even more welcome when it isn't in order," he chuckled.

Angela waved, "If you need anything, just call the desk."

"Wonderful. May your heart be glad."

Angela smiled and closed the door.

Kid unpacked four boxes before lunch. He arranged his music box collection on the corner shelf. He opened a favorite lacquered box and listened to it play 'The Music of the Night' from *Phantom of the Opera*. Closing the lid he pulled on his red and white plaid jacket and strolled down the hall. The dining room buzzed with table talk. Kid paused to survey the gray heads sitting at tables and wound his way through the chairs, smiling as he went.

He found his assigned table where a lady sat sipping coffee. She reminded Kid of a sixth grade school teacher he once had. Her hair was pulled tight in a bun. She eyed Kid over her bifocals suspiciously.

"Good day," he said. "I believe I'm to join you for lunch."

She held out her hand. "I'm Mabel Brown."

Kid sat down next to her.

"Excuse me," she said. "That is Trudy's place."

"Oh, I'm so sorry." Kid moved to the next chair. "My name is Kingsley Isaac Darlington, but I'm called Kid."

Mabel glanced toward the door.

"Do you whistle?" asked Kid.

Mabel stared at Kid. "What an odd question?" she remarked.

Kid smiled. "I'm sorry. It's just that you remind me of a school teacher I once had who whistled."

"I was never a school teacher. And if I had been I certainly would not have whistled," she snapped. Mabel peered across the dining room. "Here comes Trudy."

Kid noticed a short, round figure meandering in their direction like a pin-ball in a pin-ball machine. She arrived breathless and Kid rose to greet her, "How do you do? I'm Kid and very happy to meet you."

Trudy plopped in the chair next to Mabel. "You're new," she said. "And you're sitting in Arnold's seat."

"Oh, I've done it again," Kid apologized. He moved over. "Do I finally have it right?" He laughed.

"Well, Mr. ah…," began Trudy.

"Please, call me Kid," he said.

"Well, Mr. Kid, none of us is perfect. We're all getting on, as you can see. There are dinosaurs at every table." Trudy turned to Mabel. "And how are you, dear? Where is Arnold? Late as usual, I suppose."

"Here he comes," said Mabel. "He's using his cane today."

Arnold limped toward their table. His large western belt-buckle reflected the light as he approached.

"Good morning, dear," said Trudy.

Arnold grunted. "It's not a good morning and don't call me, dear." He folded himself into the chair without looking at Kid.

Kid grinned in his direction and offered his hand. "I'm Kid and I'm very happy to meet you."

"Saw you arrive," said Arnold. He looked at the table and did not offer to return Kid's handshake. "Where's the bland grub?"

"You mustn't swear, dear," said Trudy.

Arnold glared at her. "I wasn't swearing. I said bland."

"Oh," said Trudy. "Sounded like damn to me."

"Here's lunch," said Mabel.

Ham sandwiches and tomato soup were placed before everyone but Kid. He asked for peanut-butter and jelly and the kitchen happily made the concession. They ate in silence for a few minutes.

"Look at that, will you," said Kid, and pointed to a robin near the window.

"God," said Arnold. "I hope you're not one of those happy-go-lucky the world-is-my-oyster sort of guys."

"I'm afraid I am," said Kid. "I can't help myself. I live on the bright side."

"Egad," said Arnold. He slurped his soup and scowled across the table.

"Well, I think it's nice," said Trudy. "Birds are God's creatures too."

"Then why doesn't God tell them to quit crapping on the benches?" asked Arnold.

"I may take a walk after lunch," said Kid.

"You do that," suggested Arnold. "They play bumper-cars around here. And they don't stop for senility."

In a few weeks Kid's cheerfulness began to spread through the halls of Mayfair Assisted Living. The staff smiled at one another. Mayfair residents knocked frequently on Kid's door.

Angela stopped at his room on days when she didn't clean.

"What's that smell?" she asked one day.

"That is Jasmine incense," said Kid. "Do you like it?"

"I love it," she said.

Kid took an incense burner and two sticks of Jasmine from a shelf and handed them to her. "These are for you," he said.

"Oh, I couldn't," she objected.

"You must, it smells good and I have more than I need."

Larry, from laundry visited Kid to play checkers. Lou, in the kitchen brought donuts for coffee on Monday morning. The activities director, Ray Thomas, picked Kid's brain for new ideas.

Mrs. Palmer surprised Kid one day in the hallway and called out, "May your heart be glad."

Kid's room swarmed with activity. Residents gathered in the evening to hear Kid read aloud from his favorite children's books. Each one began to anticipate when Kid would select one of their favorite stories.

"Are you going tonight?"

"Can't go tonight."

"What's he reading?"

"It's the Velveteen Rabbit."

"Damn, that's my favorite."

At times a staff member would knock quietly on the door: "Kid, can I talk to you?" Kid extended a hand and listened to their anger or resentment.

Everyone seemed happier; all except for his dining-room companions. Not one of them showed the slightest hint of enjoying life.

One sunny afternoon, Kid entered the dining room and said, "What a beautiful day!" A barrage of complaints issued like shrapnel across the table.

"What's so beautiful about it?" asked Trudy. "We're dried decaying bones and no matter what the Bible says they'll never connect again neck-bone to the back-bone."

"It can't be that bad," offered Kid.

"Don't mind her," said Mabel. "She lost big on the horses today."

Kid smiled. "So, you play the horses?"

Trudy scowled and reached for the salt. "Why don't they salt the food, for God's sake?"

"It's for your own good," suggested Mabel.

Trudy banged the shaker on the table.

"I've had a migraine for nine days," said Arnold.

"May your hearts be glad," said Kid soothingly.

Silent resentment spread over the table like spilt decaf. Kid munched his pre-ordered peanut-butter and jelly sandwich and smiled in hope of defusing the tension. Arnold pinned Kid with bullet eyes. "You're a pain in the butt. Why don't you grow up and act your age?" He popped out of his chair and stomped from the room.

Mabel reprimanded Kid with a glance.

"I'm sorry," he said. "But I just can't apologize—for happiness."

"We all have days when we're out-of-sorts," said Mabel.

"Of course," said Kid. "I'm just concerned that Arnold fills his calendar with such days."

"I enjoy life most days," offered Trudy, "except when the damn horses won't run."

"Now, hold your horses," Kid began. He immediately realized it was the wrong thing to say. He could not tell Trudy it was her own fault for gambling. Trudy stared at Kid. She stood abruptly and poked a finger across the table. "I'm from Las Vegas," she said. "I know about gambling. Get off my back." And she, too stomped from the room.

Kid pulled his ear and smiled at Mabel.

"I think Trudy has a problem," said Mabel. "There's no getting through to her. I've tried. Besides, most of the time she's happy. Just don't mention horses, gambling, chocolate, her weight, or her daughter."

"What about her daughter?" asked Kid.

"She doesn't visit as often as Trudy would like," explained Mabel.

"We all have our burdens," said Kid.

"We do indeed," said Mabel. "We're looking over our shoulders while buzzards gather in the rafters." She stood and walked away, leaving Kid by himself. He looked out the window at the flowering rhododendron and sipped his juice.

That afternoon Kid picked up his hat and walked to the river. He sat on a bench in the park and watched the children in the playground. Kid laughed and clapped his hands. "That's wonderful, truly wonderful," he shouted.

His show of delight attracted the attention of three mothers sitting nearby. A mother in a blue blouse whispered to a mother in a white blouse, who whispered to the mother in the red blouse. Kid had a vision of the American flag accusing him of something. He wondered if happiness and enthusiasm always invited whispers. He took a deep breath and stepped to the water. Kid sat on a rock and removed his socks and shoes. He waded in the water and felt the wet earth recede under his feet. *Why do I do to invite suspicion?* he wondered.

Kid returned to the rock and dried his feet. He replaced his socks and shoes and nodded in the direction of the mothers. Returning to Mayfair, Kid pulled his room-key from his pocket.

He paused and continued down the hall to Arnold's room. Kid knocked. There was no answer.

He tried again. The door opened a crack and Arnold glared out at Kid.

"What do you want?" he asked.

"I just dropped by for a visit," said Kid.

Arnold hesitated and opened the door. He took his seat in the rocker in front of the television. Arnold waved Kid to a place on the sofa. "I don't much like being interrupted. I was watching an old episode of *Gunsmoke*."

"Oh yes, James Arness, isn't it?"

Arnold nodded. "I like old westerns." He rocked back and forth in his rocker and tapped his fingers on the arm of the chair.

"What else do you like to do?" asked Kid.

"I read a little." Arnold paused, "Louie L'amour."

"He's good," said Kid.

Arnold nervously scanned the room and looked toward the window.

"Nice day out," offered Kid.

"Means nothing," mumbled Arnold.

"You get out much?" said Kid.

"Not much." Arnold tapped his bad leg.

"Ah," said Kid. "I understand. It's hard to get around."

"You could say that." Arnold paused, "Kicked by too many damn cows."

Kid winced. "That hurts."

"Means nothing," said Arnold.

Kid walked to the door. "Come to my place sometime and bring *Gunsmoke*."

Arnold flicked a hand in his direction. "Me and the tooth-fairy," he said under his breath.

In his room, Kid stood before the window. *They weren't bad people. Eating together brings out the worst in them. Mabel turns into a pedagogue. Trudy demands constant attention.*

Arnold likes to irritate everyone. Kid took a deep breath. *And there's me, the happiness rabbit plopped down in the middle of a briar patch. Maybe I'm just missing my friends in Turner's Grove and my morning coffee at the Broken Star.* He decided to try an experiment.

Mabel, Trudy, and Arnold arrived for dinner to find Kid's chair empty.

"Where's Mr. Happy?" asked Arnold.

"Now, be kind," said Mabel.

"Here he comes," said Trudy.

Kid sat down quietly and sighed. Mabel shot him a concerned look. "Are you alright?"

Kid nodded.

"You're limp as a rubber glove," said Trudy.

Arnold stared in Kid's direction.

The meatloaf was served and Mabel said, "Doesn't this smell good?"

Kid picked at his food.

"You're coming down with something," said Trudy.

"I'm fine," said Kid. "Just a little tired."

After dinner, Mabel walked Kid back to his room. He unlocked the door.

"I'll come in and see that you're settled," she said.

"There's no need. I'll be alright."

"I'll just see that you're comfortable." She led Kid to his chair. "Can I get you anything?"

"I don't know what it would be," he said.

There was a knock on the door and Trudy brought in a bottle of sherry." "This will perk you up," she said.

Arnold knocked at the door and hesitated before coming into the room. With his eyes on the carpet he handed Kid a copy of *Gunsmoke*.

Kid nodded a thank you.

They stood quietly for a minute. "I suppose I'm out of sorts, today," said Kid.

"Why don't we all watch *Gunsmoke*?" said Trudy.

Arnold pulled over a chair from the table. Mabel sat on the couch. Trudy found glasses in the cupboard and poured everyone a glass of sherry. Arnold slid the cassette into the VCR and sat back to hear James Arness say, "Kitty, have you seen Doc?"

Kid smiled and enjoyed the company.

A week later, Trudy arrived last at the breakfast table. Mabel and Arnold were waiting.

"The place is like a morgue," said Arnold.

Trudy stared at him. "You haven't heard."

"Heard what?" asked Mabel.

"Kid had a stroke last night and died this morning."

"Arnold pulled a handkerchief from his pocket and grabbed his cane. He left the table quickly as the women looked after him.

Mabel sat in silence. "I don't know what to say. He was a person you never expected to die. I can't believe it. I'm going to my room."

The shock of Kid's death plunged Mayfair into silence. It was as if a pall had been dropped over the entire building.

That afternoon Angela stopped at Kid's room to clean. Larry from laundry followed her inside. "I can't believe it," he said. "He was such a wonderful man."

Trudy heard the voices and entered with Mabel. "We just wanted to leave some flowers," Mabel sobbed.

"Sit down, dear," said Trudy. "Is it okay if we stay a while?" she asked Angela.

"Of course, I'll wait on the cleaning."

Lou brought pastries and coffee. Mabel strolled to the shelf of music boxes and opened the one with the dancer on top. The room filled with sounds of *The Music Box Dancer*. People listened and smiled.

Mrs. Palmer entered and pulled a children's book from the shelf. "I remember when Kid first came," she said.

There was a tentative knock and Arnold walked in holding an episode of *Gunsmoke*.

Those who could stay watched Doc tip back a jigger of whiskey. Gaiety filled the room. Laughter came from the table near the window as a Lego tower spilled onto the floor. Checkers were aligned for a game and stories about Kid circulated through the room.

As the dinner hour grew near, residents and staff returned to their rooms and jobs. Mabel, Trudy, and Arnold were the last to leave.

Arnold stopped and picked up a Lego from the table and stuffed it in his pocket. He read the sign above the door, *May your Heart be Glad.*

"Dam foolishness," he mumbled and pulled the door shut behind him.

Faces From a Broken Star

CHAPTER TWELVE

Give It to the River

Allie Carroll sat by the Blue River with her journal. The words flowed easy today like the river. The morning was warm for late September. In the stillness she heard the willow leaves falling lightly to the ground. Winter could not be far off. The river ran low as if it, too, were tired.

Allie longed for the first snow. She wanted to sit by the fire and soak up the warmth. She longed to disappear into the folds of an afghan. She opened the journal and began to write.

"I do not want to remember what life was like before coming here. As a young child I played with alphabet blocks, trying to make words out of the letters. But there was always a letter missing. I'd get so angry and kick the blocks across the room. That's how I feel now. Nothing makes sense. I want to kick out against the world."

Allie closed the journal and laid it on the log where she sat. She stood and stretched her lanky body toward the morning sun. She smoothed her long black hair into a waterfall, splashing it over her shoulders. Her hazel eyes glowed defiantly. She pressed her lips tightly together, determined not to think. What good were words or thoughts on a day like this?

Returning to her journal, Allie wrote: "*Why am I so afraid? Maybe if I would do something foolish for once.*"

She'd found a secluded place along the river. The deep pool under the trees seemed hidden and safe. The spot was sheltered from passing cars. Why couldn't she unbutton her white blouse and slip out of her sandals? Why couldn't she lay her clothes on the log and enjoy the soothing water over her naked body? Allie glanced upriver. She turned and scanned along the river bank as far as she could see. Should she? Dare she? It was no use after what happened. She was too afraid.

Allie kicked off her sandals and moved to the edge of the river. She stepped to the water and felt the river flow over her feet. Her thoughts wandered to the stories of voyeurs hiding in the bushes. She listened for noises in the woods and waded into the water.

The river reached her ankles and she felt her skin tingle. A breeze swept through the trees, sending saffron leaves over the water. Allie raised her hands into the filtered sunlight like a child and began to catch the leaves in the air. She wished she were a child again.

Allie stepped from the pool and sat on the log to dry her feet. Then she stretched out on the log and let the quiet surround her. This was how she wanted to be. She shut her eyes until a breeze tickled her skin. Allie sat up and opened her journal.

"*I do not want to remember what life was like before coming here.*" Was it okay not to remember? How could she ever forget?

She could not forget. Allie closed the journal. She couldn't escape the filthy hands, the fetid breath. She glanced from the page to the moving river, recalling the train moving steadily over the tracks from the east only a few days ago. The window in the passenger's car had framed the countryside through New York, Massachusetts, and the midwest. Each scene from her window painted a new landscape, carrying her away. "Leave it all behind," she'd whispered. She was running away. Could she leave her life behind? The train's window turned dark as night came on and Allie saw her tired, fearful eyes staring back at her.

The leaves fluttered and Allie felt a slight chill. With her journal in one hand she slipped on her sandals and walked to Aunt Jen's car. It was time to get back. Aunt Jen, now in her eighties, had offered her a place to stay. "You will find it quiet in Turner's Grove," she'd said. "We're a small town and sometimes as dry as toast, but it's safe. We can breakfast at the Broken Star Café. You enjoyed that last time you were here."

"That's fine, Aunt Jen. Safe is what I need."

As Allie approached the house she could see smoke rising from the chimney. She remembered a line from Wordsworth: *'Smoke sent up in silence among the trees.'* Aunt Jen often lit a fire in early fall to cut the chill. Allie entered through the back door. She took a deep breath and savored the smell of fresh coffee. She poured herself a cup and went into the living room to sit near the fire.

"Did you have a nice time, dear?" asked Aunt Jen.

"Very nice," said Allie. She smiled at her aunt.

"I know that smile. What have you been up to?"

Allie sipped her coffee and eyed her aunt. "You know me too well. You've always been able to tell when I've done something naughty."

"I suppose I have," said Aunt Jen. "I hope you weren't too naughty."

Allie regarded her aunt. "I didn't do anything. But I wanted to go skinny-dipping in the worst way."

Aunt Jen sipped her coffee and grinned. "Why didn't you? When we lived closer to the river, I used to skinny-dip all the time."

Now it was Allie's turn to smile. "You did?"

"Of course, I went at night in the moonlight. I was never brave enough to go in the morning." She laughed. "One night I heard rustling in the bushes. It scared me half to death. I thought it was a bear." She sipped her coffee. "I remember the moon was bright on the water, but the trees were in shadow. I knew something or someone was watching. I sank beneath the water and waited. It got real quiet, the kind of quiet you hear when you know something is wrong."

"What was there, Aunt Jen?"

"Well, I didn't know at the time. After a while I got cold and quick as a grasshopper, I dressed and skedaddled home. I was about twelve then and our house was not far from the river. The next week at school I received a note from a boy named Ronny Snoops. It had a moon drawn on it. I knew then who'd been in the bushes. I hoped he got an eyeful."

"Did you stop going to the river?"

"No, but I was careful." Aunt Jen stared into the fire. "When I was a couple of years older, Ronny asked me to go to the movies in Presser. I told him I'd rather go skinny-dipping and he was welcome to come along."

"You didn't!"

"I did. You should have seen his face. You'd of thought he received a birthday wish right there. I told him to meet me at nine o'clock on Tuesday night. What I didn't tell him was that my pa took his bath in the river on Tuesdays."

"Aunt Jen, you didn't."

"That night I sat on the porch and waited. I could hear my pa splashing in the water. Then I heard Ronny whispering real loud from the woods, 'Allie, is that you? I'm naked and I'm coming in.' For a while it was so still I could hear my heart laughing. Then there was a splash and loud cussing like the devil had crawled out of the earth. I suppose Ronny thought so, too, for I saw him streaking through the trees in the moonlight like an albino deer."

"Aunt Jen, that was so mean."

"I guess it was. But he deserved it."

Allie stared into the fire. Aunt Jen chucked to herself.

"Now, dear," she said. "We need to talk. It's best to get it out. You can't keep something caged up that doesn't want to be caged. Tell me what happened that makes you want to hide out in Turners Grove."

Allie lifted her hand to her throat and felt the skin on her neck. She could almost feel the man's fingerprints. She'd tried to forget his nails digging into her skin. Following the incident she filled her days with work to keep busy. She took sleeping pills at night. But there was no memory eraser. She woke every morning with the same fear. Allie lifted her eyes to Aunt Jen.

"How does a person forget when something awful happens, Aunt Jen?"

"Tell me about it," said Aunt Jen, softly.

"I was so happy living in my apartment and spending time with my friends after my divorce. I loved my work. I was no longer responsible for cooking meals or being there for a man who no longer loved me."

Allie peered into the empty coffee cup. She raised her eyes to the fire.

"My routine was to run through Benton Park early in the morning before breakfast. Others ran that time of day. It didn't seem risky. On this particular morning a big man jumped me from behind some bushes. He grabbed me by the arms and pushed me into the undergrowth. His bulk was on top of me before I could think. The man had one hand on my throat and tried to hold me down with the other. I screamed and flailed with one arm. His weight was so heavy on my legs that I couldn't kick, but I fought and fought. He slapped me across the face to shut me up. I screamed and struck out with my fist."

"You must have been terrified," said Aunt Jen.

"I was lucky. A man and a woman came running along the path. They must have heard me scream and shouted in our direction. The man pushed himself off me and ran across the park. The couple helped me up and asked if I was hurt. They took me to a bench and used their cell phone to call the police." Allie paused. "That was pretty much it. I answered questions and gave a description as best I could. The police found a knife nearby that must have belonged to the man. I'm sure he would have used it on me if he hadn't dropped it."

Aunt Jen watched Allie's eyes fill with tears. She rose from her chair and put her arms around her niece. After a few minutes, Allie wiped her eyes. "I've had nightmares ever since. I wake up in the night and can't move my legs. I feel the man's weight on me and his fingers around my throat."

"Let me refill your cup, dear." Aunt Jen moved to the kitchen. In a few minutes she was back. "Now I want to tell you a story."

Aunt Jen returned to her chair and peered into the fire. "This is a family story and not a very nice one. But it may help. When I was just a few years past my skinny-dipping nights, I was cornered by a family friend. Don't ask me who, I won't tell you that. It happened when I was out for a walk in the woods. My mother and father found out about it, and told the man they wouldn't press charges if he promised never to come to their house again. But the damage was done. He pushed me against a tree and kissed me hard and I felt his hands on my body. I was scared."

"For a long time I felt dirty inside. No matter how hard I scrubbed my body, I couldn't get clean. It was like I was dirty all over. I imagined the man's fingers had become mice crawling over my body. I know it sounds silly. I'd wake up in the dark, screaming."

Allie stared at her aunt. She brushed away the tears from her own eyes. Finally, she managed, "Oh, Aunt Jen."

"I was terrified. For some time I couldn't even look at a man. I didn't think I would ever let a man touch me again. I seldom went to town. When I did I walked on the other side of the street with my head down to avoid people. I can tell you it was a dark time in our family."

"Well, like you, I tried to forget. 'Just get over it,' I said to myself. Then I went to stay with my wise old gran. She didn't have much schooling, but she knew a few things. I cried and cried. 'I don't know what to do about the mice,' I sobbed."

"What did she say?" asked Allie.

"She put her arms around me and looked me in the eye. 'You must give it to the river,' she said. I must have stopped crying and looked at her like a dumb fly. But she said it again, 'You must give it to the river.' 'What do you mean, Gran,' I asked? 'You must go to the river and hold your hands out over the water. You can't keep it inside you. It will get worse and you'll always feel dirty inside. You must give it all to the river.'"

"'How do I do that, Gran?' I asked."

"You go down to the river every day and you hold your hands over the water. You listen to your breathing. Let the enemy thoughts pour out of you. You must imagine all that's dirty leaving your body and falling into the water. You must imagine the mice running out your fingers into the water. Let the river carry them away to the sea. It's the only way. Give it to the river.'" Aunt Jen got up and went to put another log on the fire. She returned to her chair and sat back comfortably.

"I know it sounds like one of those home-grown remedies you'd hear from a street peddler; or worse, a witch."

"Did it work, Aunt Jen?"

"It did work. It took time. I had to go to the river over and over again. And that's what I did. Every day I went to one spot and opened my hands. I imagined the dirty stuff falling into the water and saw the mice caught in the rapids. I let go and let go and let go."

"Then one day I opened my hands and there was nothing left. I guess the river got tired of them, too, and sent it all downstream. I don't know. One day I just knew they had gone. I was cleansed by the water. The river was running pure and the sun bounced off the surface like freedom's cry. I gave thanks right then and there for the river's tender cleansing."

That night in bed Allie thought about her aunt's story. It seemed so bizarre. What had she to lose? Early the next morning she picked Aunt up Jen's keys from the kitchen counter and drove to the river. She found the log where she'd sat the day before. Allie checked the trees and walked up and down the river bank. It was cooler than yesterday, but the sun was warm on her face.

She removed her sandals and stepped into the water. Allie felt the cool water encircle her feet. She closed her eyes and listened to the bird song and how the river rippled over the rocks. She heard a twig snap and looked up. It was nothing. Allie raised her arms to the morning sun.

She dropped her hand to her skin where the attacker's fingers had tightened around her throat. Allie lifted the prints off her skin and turned them over to the river. As she bent down Allie let the water wash over her fingers. "Carry the ugly things away," she whispered.

She closed her eyes in the bright sunlight and stared into the dark eyes of the man with determination. Allie walked farther into the river and felt the water on her legs. She listened to her breathing and waited. Turning her hands toward the water she let go of the man, the knife, the fingers.

She remembered the small paper boats her father used to make when she was a child. She placed her fear in an imaginary boat and bent to place it in the water. Her eyes followed the vessel downstream and watched it careen around rocks and follow the current. "Away, away, away," she whispered.

Stepping from the water Allie sat on the log as before, letting the sun dry her legs. She opened her journal: *"I can remember what my life was like before coming to Turner's Grove."* Below the lines she wrote: *"In this quiet place, I will let life begin again."*

CHAPTER THIRTEEN

After the Wedding Vows

Harriet Benson glanced at the television on the back seat of the Chevette. She raised her eyes to the highway. No one was following. She turned to the man next to her with his hands on the steering wheel, and screamed.

The embryo of Harriet's scream was conceived three years earlier when she met Jerry Benson in Tiny's Tavern. He'd been working a backhoe in Turner's Grove for about a week. The Baptist Church was putting in a new parking lot and had hired JJ Construction from Presser to do the work.

Harriet, thirty-five, short, with bouncy red hair had always been easy to persuade, She had excepted an invitation to dinner with Jerry at the Broken Star Café. They continued to see each other during the weeks Jerry worked in Turner's Grove. After dinner they'd often go to her place to watch movies. One night they stayed awake for a Gregory Peck marathon. Between *Roman Holiday* and *Spellbound* Jerry popped corn, popped a can of beer and popped the question. Harriet, operating on the love is blind principle, said yes.

Before anyone in Turner's Grove knew about the engagement, Harriet had run off with Jerry to get married.

Neither Jerry nor Harriet belonged to a church. The wedding

ceremony took place near Beatrice at The Church of Common Faith. Perhaps Harriet should have noticed the gleam in Jerry's eye when the minister said, "I, a minister of The Church of Common Faith, pronounce you husband and wife." They arrived at the Pixy Motel and watched *Dancing With The Stars* on the television. The next morning they continued south and stopped for breakfast at a country café in Kansas. The trouble began over ham and eggs.

"I could do that," said Jerry.

"You can do what?"

"I could be a minister and marry people."

"You!" said Harriet. She smiled and took a bite of toast.

Jerry sliced his ham.

The next night while staying at a Holiday Inn Jerry used the complementary computer to find The Church of Common Faith on-line. The website directed him to an internet course offered by The Church of Common Faith College. In the next month Jerry completed courses in Bible, Preaching, Worship, Counseling, and Administration. He withdrew the last of their savings and paid for a Certificate of Ordination that read:

Rev. Jerry Benson
Ordained July 1, 2010
Church of Common Faith

From a list provided by the college, Jerry received an appointment to a church in Blip, Arkansas. Harriet, now Mrs. Rev. Jerry Benson, found herself on the way to a town with one barber shop, a tavern, and small grocery store.

Jerry lacked in almost everything but nerve. He quickly found an on-line sermon source and began reading canned sermons on Sunday. The sermons required almost no preparation. This gave Jerry time to watch television. The people in Blip, Arkansas, were not delighted to find the T.V. on in the Pastor's office. Reverends were supposed to be prayerful and open to visits from their parishioners. They found this impossible unless they wanted to talk about *American Idol* or *Survivor*.

The church council was finally forced to ask Jerry to seek another position. He disconnected his television and loaded the Chevette with their few belongings and headed to the next parish.

Although Jerry was short on common sense, he wasn't stupid. He soon saw that diplomacy was required. He decided to teach a Bible Study from a mail-order source. He chose a course he called 'Understanding Revelations.'

Offering a Bible class and hiding his television behind a curtain in his study enabled Jerry to stay in Token, Oklahoma, for eleven months and fourteen days. His deception worked well until once again Jerry's addiction to television caught up with him. Before long he and Harriet were driving away, this time to Ma'ii', New Mexico.

Ma'ii' is the name for coyote in Navajo. To Jerry's way of thinking, this was an omen. He would be as sly as a coyote. He engaged Harriet as church secretary. Harriet thought this might be a way to establish some permanency. She sat at the reception desk and handled calls.

"Yes, the pastor is in. Just a moment, please."

"Sorry, he has someone with him. Can I take a message?"

"He's quite busy this week. Let me look at his appointment book."

It was perfect. Jerry could sit behind his desk with ear phones and watch his favorite movies.

But coyotes, no matter how clever, get caught. Jerry was trapped while Harriet was at Video Fever getting the latest movies. The poacher who caught Jerry was none other than the bank manager, Sylvester Trambo, who was also president of the church council.

Not only did Sylvester open the door and see the television, but Jerry was watching *Darlings of Twilight*. Sylvester slammed the office door and called a meeting of the church council. This was the final insult for Harriet and brings us back to the beginning of our story.

The television was on the back seat of the Chevette. Jerry was driving west through the New Mexico desert. Harriet saw the television in the back seat and lifted her eyes to see if anyone was following.

She screamed. Her eyes no longer recognized Jerry. In his place a television set was driving the car. Jerry pulled to the side of the road and watched Harriet open the car door and run into the saguaro. He was too stunned to move when a police car pulled in behind him.

The officer saw a woman running through the cactus and a television in the back seat. He handcuffed Jerry and put him in the back seat of the police car with the television. Another officer ran to gather the pieces of Harriet Benson. A back-up unit arrived and wild-eyed Harriet is helped inside the squad car and taken to the hospital.

The story makes its rounds in Turner's Grove and those at the Broken Star Café asked how the story ended? Was Jerry Benson found innocent of driving Harriet mad? Did he spend days and nights beside Harriet's hospital bed? Did he promise to go to weekly meetings of TWA, Television Watchers Anonymous?

Did Harriet recover her sanity and find a job as an aide in a care facility? People, like elephants, can have long memories. So it was with Harriet. She decided that her marriage to Jerry could not be turned on and off like a television.

Harriet left Jerry. She moved back to Nebraska to an apartment in Presser. She no longer attended church. Harriet avoided the long wall of televisions on display at Sears. According to Doris at the Broken Star Café, Harriet still thinks marriages are performed by phony clergy who have secretaries to protect them from church council presidents.

Harriet found Joan to share her apartment. They are perfectly happy without men in their lives. When Harriet wakes in the night, screaming, Joan is able to convince her that there is no television behind the curtains. Harriet turns over and goes back to sleep.

CHAPTER FOURTEEN

Cordon Bleu

Cordell Celestine sat on a stump by the Blue River, his violin on his lap. The glint from the sun reflected off the river and caught the patina of his instrument. Cordell blinked. He ran a hand over the violin. How could he love an object so much and find it was so difficult to love people? The sunspots shimmering off the water blinded him for a moment. He glanced away to the shaded trees across the river and lifted the violin to play.

"Why doesn't Cordell Celestine speak to his mother?" Doris asked Rick one night as they closed the Broken Star Cafe.

"Beats me," said Rick. "I've heard rumors, but that's all they are."

Cordell Celestine lived on the Blue River south of town. His mother, M. Celestine, lived north of town near Turner Lake. Raymond Peterson had met M. Celestine in France during the war. She was a single mother with an infant. They married after the war and moved back to the states. Following Raymond's death M went back to using her maiden name, Celestine. She'd lived the last forty years alone.

At seventy-five, Cordell could still recall his step-father's disappointment. "Why do you play that thing? What's wrong with sports?"

Cordell thought helping on the farm might please his step father, but his efforts were never enough. The decision to send him away to school was made one Sunday afternoon by his mother. Raymond argued with Cordell. He'd been drinking and marched into Cordell's room while Cordell was practicing. His step father grabbed the violin and crushed it beneath his feet. From that moment Cordell hated his step father. He was glad to be sent away to school.

Raymond Peterson died a short time later. Cordell didn't return to the house of pain. He made a brief appearance at the funeral and continued with school. Cordell studied music and became a concert violinist. He traveled and played professionally until he retired after a long career.

Cordell moved to a cabin outside Turner's Grove. He hadn't spoken to his mother in ten years. She still lived on the farm north of town. No one in Turner's Grove knew the reason for the estrangement. As time passed M. Celestine became embittered toward her son.

At the entrance to Cordell's drive stood a sign with faded blue letters *Cordon Bleu*. The words suggested to many that this might be the residence of a master chef. Originally the French moniker was given to members of the Order of the Holy Ghost during the Bourbon monarchy who wore the blue ribbon as decoration. Cordell chose the name because of its proximity to his own and his place on the Blue River.

Cordon Bleu also referred to a person distinguished in any field. This was true of Cordell. But for him the sign simply marked the place to turn off the highway to his cabin.

As a master violinist Cordell gave back to the community by teaching violin. It was an invaluable gift to the people of Turner's Grove and occasionally he was persuaded to play at local benefits. Cordell lived a quiet life by the river immersed in his music and his library.

Books were Cordell's other passion. Music was the first sound he heard in the morning. The closing of a book was the last sound he heard at night. Cordell was not lonely. Music and books were enough.

Cordell drove to town on Monday evenings in his 1955 Volkswagen bus. He stopped at the Broken Star Café and read at the same table the Professor used on Tuesday mornings. The fact that the professor and he had never met surprised many people.

Doris began calling the booth, the Library. As Cordell sat at the table one night, she moved the salt and pepper shakers, arranged the catsup, and poked under the table.

"Did you lose something?" asked Cordell.

"No," said Doris. "I'm just curious about this booth. What is it that makes everyone who sits here want to read?"

Cordell laughed. "Doris, it isn't the light I can tell you that. It must be the good coffee." He visited town on Monday nights because Charlie Little's bookstore stayed open late.

Doris wondered if Cordell's choice of day might have to do with his family quarrel. His younger half sister, Alice, and her husband, Bradley ran the *Turner Reporter*. Because of their place in the business community, Cordell limited his visits to when the newspaper office was closed.

Cordell loved his sister, but she was a nagging reminder that he should visit his mother.

On the day Cordell sat by the river and played the Andante from Concerto Number 2 in D Minor by Mozart, it was quiet. The music lifted into the air. He imagined that the river picked up the accompaniment as an orchestra might have in the concert hall. The soft tones of the violin and the ripple of water seemed to blend into a perfect moment of peace. Perhaps it reminded him the past. With his eyes closed he could almost picture himself on stage again. He felt the sun wash over him like the an audience's applause.

But peace was not always at hand. Two days a week parents brought children for lessons. While their children played, a mother or father sat by the river or in their cars. The lessons lasted a half hour and parents didn't seem to mind the wait. Most knew the house was small and their presence would be a distraction on a student.

Children who took lessons talked about Cordell on their ride home.

"Dad, Mr. Celestine calls his violin, Cordelia."

"Does he now?"

"He's so gentle with it. He says an instrument is like a living thing and scolds us if we're not careful with our own violin. 'Treat it like a friend and it will sing for you,' he says."

"I'm sure Mr. Celestine understands the value of a violin," said one mother.

Her son answered, "I know, but it's so strange."

"In what way, dear?"

"When Mr. Celestine begins a lesson he lifts his violin from the case and stands quietly. Then he gently wipes the violin with a special cloth. He picks it up and tunes the instrument. Finally, he carries it to the window and whispers, 'Sing to me.'"

"Does the violin sing to him?" asked his mother.

"Yes, it does. Mr. Celestine plays a short piece to show us how we might play one day."

"Mr. Celestine is a great violinist. You are lucky to have lessons from him."

When Cordell came to the end of the Andante he laid the instrument on his lap. He listened to the applause of running water until the sound of car tires on the gravel drive startled him.

Cordell knew the visitor by the sound of the engine. He heard Alice shut the car door and walk toward him. He continued to stare out at the river with the violin in his lap.

"Good morning," said Alice. "How are you?"

"I'm fine," said Cordell. "Would you like a cup of coffee?"

"No thank you, I can't stay. I know you don't want to hear this, but I must say it. Will you do me this one favor?"

Cordell looked down into the hollow sound box of his violin. He felt the emptiness inside himself. A knot formed in his stomach.

"I love you and mother," said Alice. "This is hard for me. Will you listen?" Alice wiped teas from her eyes.

Cordell did not look up, but nodded.

"Mother is celebrating her one hundredth birthday next week.

We're having a luncheon celebration at the Broken Star Café. I know it's a lot to ask, but will you come?"

Cordell did not answer. He waited, silent, unable to speak. Time passed. He was conscious of the river sweeping by.

Alice returned to her car and drove away. Pollen dust blew over the river from the trees and Cordell covered the violin with his upper body. When the dust settled he caressed the instrument. He raised his eyes once again into the light and felt his own tears flow.

CHAPTER FIFTEEN

Sara

"You seem a little glum," remarked Kate.

It was a Saturday morning in late July. Sara and Kate ordered coffee at the Broken Star Cafe.

Sara glanced out the window. "It's silly, I know, but I find myself thinking about Jason."

"That guy on the Harley?"

Sara nodded, "He's too young to die."

"And too good looking," interrupted Kate.

Sara smiled, "It doesn't make sense. There are people who throw their lives away on drugs and alcohol and live to be ninety."

"Has he written?"

Sara spun her coffee cup on the table. "He sent a postcard saying he'd arrived in Seattle. He didn't give a return address. I think he has a terminal illness."

"You don't know that."

"He didn't say it in so many words. He kept saying, 'my life is on hold.' I think he has Lou Gehrig's disease."

Kate hesitated. "How long can someone live with that?"

"I'm not sure. Not long, I'd guess. Actually, we never discussed it. He seemed to want it that way."

Doris passed the table with the coffee pot. "What are the two of you up to today?"

"This and that," said Kate.

Doris refilled their cups. "Do you want something with your coffee?"

"We're fine," answered Sara.

Kate watched Doris move to the next booth. She reached in her purse for her wallet.

"Let's go to Lincoln today. I'll drive."

"Good idea. I need some office supplies."

Sara and Kate slid out of the booth and paid for their coffee. "Can we drop my car off at my house?"

Kate pulled the keys from her handbag, "I'll follow you."

Three weeks later on the first of September light poured through Sara's bedroom window. She'd finished *The Bashful Dragon* and sent it to the publisher. Sara lay in bed listening to the automatic coffee maker begin its cycle. She decided to give herself a free day and go for a walk along the river. She stepped out onto the deck. The weather was cooler now and picnickers were fewer in the park. The crows scavenged for food scraps and made a ruckus in the trees.

She returned to her bedroom, stretched, and opened the curtains. A beam of sun warmed her skin through her night gown. She pulled her robe over her gown and shuffled to the kitchen. Filling a Broken Star cup she carried it back to the deck.

Sara glanced down the valley. She paused, holding her coffee with both hands. It couldn't be, but it was. Flute music drifted up the hill. She turned her eyes to the large oak tree. The red Harley stood in the shadows. "Jason," she whispered.

Sara picked up the birding binoculars. Jason waved in her direction. Then he slipped the flute back in its case. Climbing on his bike, he looked in her direction and pointed toward town.

He started the engine and drove away.

Sara left her coffee cup on the table and dressed quickly. She backed the Jeep Cherokee down the drive. The steering wheel was cold, but her hands were sweating as she pulled into the parking lot of the Broken Star.

As she walked past the cash register, Doris nodded toward her usual table. "Someone has your booth, hun," said Doris.

"I think I know him," Sara said as she approached the table.

Jason stood up. "Good morning."

"You're certainly one for surprises."

He waited for her to take a seat and slid into the booth across from her. "I know. I have some explaining to do."

Doris brought coffee and began to pour. "Will there be anything else?"

Jason smiled. "Give us a minute." He turned to Sara. "How have you been?"

"I'm fine. I just can't believe you're here. Are you still on hold?"

Jason smiled. "Well, some things have changed."

Sara shook her head. "I mean, you left without any explanation. And then I found that book and I thought…"

"I know. I'm sorry. It was pretty abrupt and I intended to write from Seattle. Then things happened so fast and I had good news." Jason paused. He raised his eyes to Sara. "I wanted to come back and explain in person."

Doris brought menus and placed them on the table.

"Would you like something to eat," asked Jason.

Sara tapped the menu. "I'll have one blueberry pancake."

Jason handed the menus to Doris, "I'll have two of the same."

Sara gazed out the window. "I was so upset after thinking about that book you had me return to the library. I knew what it meant and I was …"

"I'm sorry." Jason reached across the table and touched Sara's wrist.

She pulled her hand back. "Excuse me a minute. I'll be back." She rose and turned toward the Ladies' Room.

When she returned, the plates were on the table.

"You okay?" asked Jason.

Sara picked up her knife and fork and began attacking the pancake. "I'm sorry. It's just such a shock. I thought …" Sara waved her knife in the air. "And now here you are in my world."

"I know."

"I guess I should be happy for you."

"When I first arrived in Turner's Grove. I was pretty focused on myself. I know that. I'd been given a pretty bad diagnosis in Minneapolis. I really thought the trip to Seattle would be my last. I was scheduled for more tests at Fred Hutchinson. That's why I didn't say too much. I didn't want sympathy."

Sara poured syrup over her pancakes. "I know, 'My life is on hold.'"

"It was a stupid thing to say. I felt so good about being here. I was torn. I kept saying to myself, if only this had happened years ago. Why now? I knew it was foolish. When I got to Seattle, they ran more tests and found the first diagnosis was wrong."

"You mean it wasn't Lou Gehrig's disease?" Sara questioned.

"It seems some of my symptoms are similar to those of other diseases which are treatable."

Sara laid down her fork and brushed her hair from her eyes. "Why couldn't you tell me?"

"I couldn't. I just couldn't. It wouldn't have been fair."

Sara sat back. "So you're telling me your life is no longer on hold."

Jason took a bite and nodded.

"It's good news, then."

"It was great news for me. When I heard the results of the tests, I couldn't believe it. I thought they'd made a mistake." He paused and pushed his plate away. "Then, like some switch had been turned on, my first thoughts returned to Turner's Grove."

Sara stared at him across the table, "Why Turner's Grove?"

Jason shrugged. "Maybe it was the rural stillness. Maybe it was your friends, or the apple pie."

"That must have been it." She smiled. "And you never read *The Bashful Dragon*."

"Actually, that's the real reason I came back. I wanted to find out how the Bashful Dragon did in preschool."

"Are you staying?"

"I've checked into the boarding house in town."

"Do you have any plans?"

Jason smiled. "I thought I'd see if Lyman's Dairy needs any help and stick around for a while."

Sara held Jason's eye. "Well, I'm on a break for a few days. Can you come to dinner tonight?"

"No, I can't. It's my turn. Is there a place in Presser or Lincoln we might go?" He hesitated. "We could pick up where we left off."

"We can't do that," said Sara.

"Why not?"

"Because when you left your life was on hold. If we go to dinner, I want to start again as if it's the first time."

Jason grinned. "I like that. All holds are off."

"That might be going too far." Sara smiled. "There is one more thing. I'll drive. I'd rather not fly through Presser on a Harley."

"Fine, I'll come by your place about six."

Sara rose and Jason picked up their checks. "I'll get these and see you this evening."

When he'd left, Doris nodded in his direction. "Where'd he come from?" she asked Sara

"From being on hold," said Sara.

CHAPTER SIXTEEN

Boston Tipps

Boston Tipps never lived in Turner's Grove. His only visit to the Broken Star Café was during that summer he came to visit his cousin, Rick Moon. But his story was discussed frequently after hours by Rick and Doris. Here is how Doris remembered his story.

Boston Tipps bit into his cheese sandwich at Founder's Park in Lincoln. The park was empty except for the lady on the opposite bench. She was a lunchtime regular who sat in the sun every day. "A mole on a bench," Boston mused to himself. The lady lifted a donut to her mouth with one puffy hand while holding a dog leash with the other.

"Curious," he thought. The cocker spaniel wasn't going anywhere. It lay in the grass like a lump of dried mustard. The dog raised its head and gazed at Boston with liquid brown eyes.

Boston stared into the dark canine pools. "You're the lazy one," the dog seemed to say.

"You're no better than me. You have sad eyes like mine, big ears, and a long nose."

Boston almost felt the leash tighten around his neck. He pulled out his watch to check the time. He needed to get back to H & S Paper Products, *Maker of All Things for Your Office*. Boston folded his lunch sack neatly into a square and slipped it in his pocket. It was time to return to the forty-story building and its mailroom in the basement.

Boston Tipps was a thin pencil of a man. In his beige clerk's uniform he blended into almost everything. He moved deliberately along the street, his ghostly reflection following him in the shop windows. Arriving at H & S, he glanced at the receptionist who did not see him and took the stairs to the basement. Boston hung his hat on the rack and opened the mail sacks that had come in his absence.

The room was bright with fluorescent lighting. Customers peeking through an open mailbox or past the service window could see Boston rub his eyes. But Boston had become invisible to most people. Young people pushed past him on the street as if he were a translucent worm crawling along the sidewalk. Visitors to the park during lunch hour considered him a regular fixture, a statue devoid of pigeons. The pretty receptionist at the front desk paid him no attention as he passed in and out of the building.

The only conversation Boston heard during the day came as questions through the service window. "Is there a package for me?" "Have you delivered anything to the third floor?" Boston bore the questions respectfully. The daily mail had dropped to a minimum of late. New technology was changing everything. The mailroom would soon be a thing of the past. Boston hoped his job would last until his retirement in six months.

At three o'clock Boston checked to see that the last of the day's mail had been delivered. He shut the service window and replaced his clerk's hat with his fedora. Locking the door behind him, Boston took the elevator to the lobby and stepped into the gray afternoon. He turned west toward his studio apartment.

But Boston was in no hurry to go home. He knew what he would find: a dark hall, the narrow stairs to the third floor, and a green door with the brass number 00 at the center. When he unlocked the door everything would be as he'd left it: the bed neatly made against one wall, the table holding the reading lamp. On the counter he'd find the hotplate for warming his soup. Nothing would have changed. Boston would stare at the walls with the single print of *The Gleaners* by Millet. He'd cross the room and pull back the curtains at the only window. The light from outside would lighten the room only slightly. In winter he would stare across the street at the flashing blue marquee of the Broadmoor Theater.

No, Boston was in no hurry to go home. He turned east and walked to Pond's Book Shop. There he found a few moments of happiness. It would have been complete happiness if he could buy the book in the glass-fronted bookcase.

Gregory Arendale Pond rose from a stool behind the counter when Boston entered. Pond, a smiling gnome of a man, watched Boston go to the bookcase and turn in his direction. Pond nodded his usual approval and watched Boston extract white gloves from his coat pocket, open the glass door, and remove a single maroon volume. He held the book as one might a crystal vase. The book's polished leather was embossed with gold vines spreading their leaves over the front and back covers. The edges were gilt and the endpapers textured the color of plums.

Boston admired the book for a long time before opening it to the title page: *Selected Poems of William Butler Yeats*. The price of $600 was penciled lightly at the top of the inside cover, a small fortune considering Boston's meager salary. Although he could not own it, he could visit it once a week at Pond's Book Shop. Each week he turned to a particular poem by Yeats:

> *Had I the heaven's embroidered cloths,*
> *Enwrought with golden and silver light,*
> *The blue and the dim and the dark cloths*
> *Of night and light and the half-light,*
> *I would spread the cloths under your feet:*
> *But I, being poor, have only my dreams;*
> *I have spread my dreams under your feet;*
> *Tread softly because you tread on my dreams.*

Gregory Pond watched as Boston whisper the words to himself and carefully replaced the volume. He closed the glass doors as if they contained the sacred *Torah* and removed his gloves. Boston stood for a moment as if in prayer and turned to Gregory Pond. He said a quiet thank you and left the shop.

To Boston Tipps, who knew little beauty or joy in his life, owning the Yeats would be like finding one of the seven cities of Cibola. On the way home Boston decided he would try to save the $600 before he retired. He would eat less and save more from his paycheck. On his return home Boston found a coffee can beneath the sink. He dropped the day's change inside the can. It was a beginning.

The weeks and months passed, as had so many years of weeks and months. Boston Tipps opened the mailroom at eight o'clock. He closed at twelve o'clock for lunch and a walk in the park. On the days when the cocker-spaniel lady sat across from him, Boston watched her hold the leash with one hand and eat her donut with the other. Always the dog's sad eyes accused him. He wondered if the dog was happy.

Each Wednesday Boston left work and visited Pond's Book Shop. He waited like a child before a candy counter until Gregory Pond nodded his approval. Boston pulled on the white gloves and gently removed the book from its shelf. By now he had memorized the poem, but it made no difference. The book itself was soft and beautiful and meant as much to him as did the poem itself. He turned to the poem and whispered the words.

> *I would spread the cloths under your feet:*
> *But I, being poor, have only my dreams;*
> *I have spread my dreams under your feet;*
> *Tread softly because you tread on my dreams.*

Boston replaced the book, thanked Gregory Pond, and stepped briskly home. He entered the narrow stairway to the third floor with new purpose. Inserting his key was like opening the door to his own safe-deposit box. The coffee can he kept on the table caught his eye. He opened the window and pulled back the curtain. Each day Boston emptied his pockets of change and added them to his savings. On Fridays he paid his rent and utilities. He subtracted the meager amount needed for food and put what was left in the can.

As the days slipped toward retirement no one commented on Boston's retirement. He continued to feel invisible, unnoticed, and unwanted. Occasionally someone would ask a question. When he wasn't busy Boston sat on a stool in the corner, much like the cocker spaniel lying in the grass in Founder's Park. Would anyone notice if he wandered away after all these years?

One evening following work Boston noticed the money in the coffee can had reached the third ring that circled the inside. He poured a cup of coffee and sat down at the kitchen table. Boston emptied the money onto the Formica top and meticulously separated the coins into their proper denominations. He laid the one's, the five's, and the ten dollar bills in appropriate piles. He began to count. His mind raced as he neared the end.

He had saved $592.82. Boston Tipps sucked in his breath. Tears rolled down his cheeks.

He didn't cry often. But tomorrow he could go to Pond's Book Shop and buy the Yeats?

The following day Boston strolled confidently to work. The hands on the clock seemed to move slower than usual. How much of his life had been lived by clock-time? At noon he thought of going to the book shop, but decided to wait until after work. The afternoon slipped by like a banana slug making its way over a sidewalk. At last it was time to lock up the mailroom. Boston had forgotten about his approaching retirement. He was too excited about the purchase of the Yeats volume.

He walked east past Baystone Bagels, Lady Marian's Boutique, and The Coffee Beanery. He entered Pond's Book Shop, holding the coffee can under his arm. Gregory Pond smiled at him and eyed the coffee can Boston placed on the counter.

"Will you take five hundred ninety-two dollars and eighty-two cents for that book?"

Gregory Pond's mouth dropped open and then closed in a frown. He looked at the coffee can and back at Boston. "I'd love to, Mr. Tipps, but I can't."

"Why not?"

"Because I sold it yesterday afternoon."

Boston stared at Gregory. He turned slowly to face the bookcase. He saw the empty space where the book had been. As if asleep he stepped to the shelf and touched the glass door. He felt tears fill his eyes. He mumbled the first line of the poem to himself, *Had I the heaven's embroidered cloths,* and drew a kleenex from his jacket pocket. Boston returned to the counter and picked up the coffee can. With his head lowered he quickly walked to the door. As he opened it he heard Gregory say, "Sorry, Mr. Tipps. If I had known…" In a daze Boston made his way back to his apartment.

By eleven o'clock that night he had been rocking in his chair for hours. He did not eat. As the room grew dark Boston moved to his bed and closed his eyes. He repeated the poem in his head and thought of the beautiful maroon leather with the embossed vines spreading their golden leaves over the cover. He gazed into the dark and fell asleep.

The next two days should have been happy ones. Boston was nearing the end of thirty years in the same job. No one seemed to notice. The questions were the same. The clerks and secretaries picked up their mail politely. The clock on the wall ticked off the same working hours. The key in the door turned the same way. The cheese sandwich at lunch tasted the same. The lady on the bench sat in exactly the same place. The cocker spaniel laid his sad head on the same paws and stared at him with the same liquid brown eyes.

Boston returned to the mailroom for his last afternoon shift. At 2:30 Mr. Chandler, the CEO for H & S Paper Products, came to the postal service window. Boston only remembered seeing Mr. Chandler twice a year as he made his semi-annual rounds. Usually he sent his personal secretary to pick up packages or mail.

"Good day, Mr. Tipps."

"Sir," replied Boston.

"I understand this is your last day."

Boston lowered his head and mumbled, "Yes, I guess it is."

Boston did not hear was the trickle of footsteps coming down the stairs or the elevators full of people descending to the basement.

"I want you to know," continued Mr. Chandler, "that we have valued your work at H & S Paper Products." Boston looked past Mr. Chandler and noticed people gathering in the room. "I doubt if you have ever been late to work," continued Mr. Chandler. "And I know you have missed very few days over the thirty years of your employment."

Boston stretched to look past Mr. Chandler to the gathering crowd.

"You have been an example to us all, Mr. Tipps. Whether you know or not, the employees of H & S Paper Products have admired your quiet diligence and commitment."

"Thank you, sir," chocked Boston.

"Ms. Rosen, may I have the package?"

Mr. Chandler took a gift-wrapped package from his secretary and handed it to Boston.

"This is a token of our appreciation and a small thank you for your work these past thirty years."

Boston took the gift with trembling hands. His fingers struggled to pull the ribbon, he managed somehow to unwrap the parcel. He lifted the maroon leather volume from the paper and raised liquid eyes to the crowd. His mouth opened as if to speak. Like the cocker spaniel in the park, he had no words. Someone in the crowd began to clap, and the room erupted in applause.

Boston, who had been invisible all his life, felt as if he had risen from the basement to the top floor of H & S Paper Products. He did not know what to do or say. He looked from the Yeats volume to the crowd and nodded.

Mr. Chandler reached for Boston's hand. Shaking it, he said once again, "Thank you, Mr. Tipps. You will be missed."

With that he left the room and the crowd made its way forward to shake the hand of the speechless, but visible, Mr. Tipps.

CHAPTER SEVENTEEN

M. Celestine

M. Celestine stared out the upstairs window. Her eyes followed the drive past the barn to the abandoned feather shop across the road. M. let out a snort. *Who'd believe there was once a business in Turner's Grove that used chicken feathers to make archery arrows?*

M. Celestine had outlived the feather shop. *I lean a little,* she thought, *but I still stand on my own foundation. I'm a century old today.* She smiled. *Life is but the click of a weaver's shuttle.* Where had she read that? The Bible she supposed. A brisk wind rattled the window panes. She glanced at the rumpled bed clothes.

Paris, where she had been born, seemed a long way from Turner's Grove. For a young girl in her twenties, coming to America had been an adventure. What a lark, the steam-ship, the train, the wagon, with "Just Married" painted on the tailgate. Raymond called her 'M' rather than Mariette, out of affection. That was how people in Turner's Grove knew her now.

Raymond died forty-five years ago. She glanced at the bed where she'd slept alone all these years. Raymond had been her only true love.

Even now, staring across the familiar pasture, she could feel his hand slide up her leg. M laughed. She was standing over the furnace grate. The warm air raised her nightgown. Still, she imagined his hand moving up her thigh as it had in Paris.

M looked over the hemlock trees that grew along the road leading to town. The barn door banged in the wind. Cordell lived somewhere south of town. She'd never been to his place. M seldom left the house. She once told Rick and Doris at the Broken Star Café that town depressed her. *The only place I find anyone younger than myself is in the Turner's Grove Cemetery, and they aren't much company.*

A dust-devil whipped across the road and up the drive. Again, warm air from the furnace sent erotic fingers up her legs. M still remembered Raymond's hand beneath the bed clothes, naughty boy. She hadn't forgotten those mornings of passionate love before work.

Raymond had never farmed. It was M herself who came from a farming family in France.

She and Crow, the hired hand did most of the farm work. Raymond owned the Turner's Grove newspaper.

She slipped on her robe and shuffled to the stairs. Holding onto the wooden rail she stepped carefully down the first step. One step at a time was all she dared now. She could hear Alice's voice, "Mom, you shouldn't live alone. There's that assisted living place in Presser."

But M. held out. The doctor said there was nothing wrong with her that a stubborn pill wouldn't cure.

She moved to the kitchen, a remodel thanks to Alice and Bradley, her son-in-law. The tile counter-top had replaced the linoleum of an earlier time. M started the coffee maker. She pulled a cup from the cupboard. Coffee in the morning, mint-chocolate after lunch, and a glass of red wine in the evening. "I'm not dead yet," she said out loud.

M slid her chair up to the old table. At least that remained. She'd gone to war to keep Alice and Bradley from tagging it for the Goodwill. The table, like her skin, bore the wrinkles and scars of time. History was carved into every scratch and coffee stain. She traced her finger along a grove.

"God M," she addressed herself, "you need to trim your fingernails.

Today's your birthday lunch at the Star. But she couldn't move.

She looked across the table where Raymond used to sit. She imagined Alice still on her right and Cordell on the left before he went away to school. The coffee pot gurgled. She'd lost them all except Alice, of course. M looked quickly at the clock above the sink. Alice would come for her at eleven.

M stepped to the stairwell and raised her eyes to the top step. She could still hear Cordell climbing the stairs, farting all the way. He was six then and when he reached the top he said, "My bum is loud, isn't it mother."

She remembered her answer, "Especially in the stairwell. But you might say excuse me."

Climbing the stairs one at a time, she stood before the mirror and appraised her thinning gray hair. "I'm sagging like the old barn," she said. "I hope I don't smell like one." M had always been tall and carried herself with dignity. Her deep brown eyes held prominence over her long nose. She slipped out of her nightgown, but avoided looking at her aging body.

Following a bath, M chose a black dress. She'd always favored dark colors. She could hear Alice's voice again, "Mother, black on your birthday!" She selected a pearl necklace, brushed her hair again, and returned down stairs to wait for Alice.

M. Celestine sat before the bow window, gazing down the drive. She thought about Crow. He'd been a good hand during his short time. Not very tall, but stocky and strong. He'd wandered from Crow Agency in Montana. He didn't fit the stereotype of an Indian.

"Just as well," thought M, Crow had offered to help one Monday afternoon on his way south. He'd run out of gas money and needed work. Raymond showed him where to sleep in the hayloft. Crow worked with a crew all day, bailing hay. He knew farming and Raymond offered him a job. Crow settled in for three years.

For a brief time Turner's Grove boasted an Indian, a black man, and one Frenchy, M laughed.

She heard the Subaru change gears over the hill. It came into view and turned up the drive. M rose from her chair and pulled on her cardigan. She checked the burners on the kitchen stove and switched off the light. Alice jumped from the car as M knew she would. M gingerly folded herself into the seat. "Watch your fingers, Mom," said Alice as she closed the door.

Alice turned the car down the drive. "How are you mom?"

"How do you mean?"

"Are you feeling okay?"

"Just fine considering I'm older than the trees."

"One hundred years. My you look good. We'll pick up Raymond on the way. He's taking the afternoon off for your birthday."

"That's decent of him. I have a bone to pick with him anyway."

"What's that mom?"

"I didn't get my paper this morning. That never used to happen when your father ran the paper."

Alice turned to her mother. "I'm sure there's an explanation. We'll see that you get one."

They drove past the abandoned feather shop south toward town. As they reached Will's Farm Supply they saw Orlin Fingerpott walking along the sidewalk. "Shouldn't he be a Ma's Grocery?" said M.

"Maybe he needs a ride," said Alice. She pulled alongside Orlin, but he waved them on.

They stopped at the *Turner's Grove Reporter*. Bradley came out the door and climbed in the back seat. "Hi mom, how do you feel?"

"Why is everyone concerned with how I feel. I may outlive you all."

"Did you take your stubborn pill today?"

"Now don't get me started," said M. "And where's my paper?"

Alice made a left turn and said, "We'll go in the Café's back door." M glanced along the storefronts. "There seem to be a lot of cars in town today. Maybe there won't be room for us."

"We've reserved a table," said Alice.

They parked and Bradley got out and opened the door for his

mother-in-law and offered her his arm. They entered the back door and Alice led her mother down the narrow hallway.

As they came to the dinning-room M blinked in the bright light. The café erupted with "Surprise!" M's legs almost buckled. Bradley led her to a center table. Everyone stood and applauded. She looked over the room and saw the whole town staring back at her. On the table was a copy of today's *Reporter* with the headlines: M. CELESTINE ONE HUNDRED YEARS OLD TODAY!

M sat down. *They hadn't forgotten.* She felt Alice stand and put her hand on her shoulder. When the applause stopped, Alice said, "Thank you all for coming. I only wish…" she began. The sweet sound of a violin came from the kitchen. No one moved. Those at the counter looked toward the swinging door. M. Celestine sat rigid and saw the door push open and Cordell came into the room still playing.

M pulled a handkerchief from her bag and wiped her eyes. When Cordell finished the piece, there was silence in the room. No one moved. Then someone clapped and the room filled with applause.

Cordell glanced at his mother with tears in his eyes. He lifted the violin and played the melody to *Happy Birthday*. On the second time through, the crowd began to sing.

Rick pushed a cart from the kitchen with a white frosted cake on it. Blue letters covered the surface with the words, *Happy Birthday M. 100 Years*. Rick bent over and kissed her on the cheek. Everyone applauded and sat down to enjoy the celebration.

Faces From a Broken Star

CHAPTER EIGHTEEN

White Iris

After twenty years of cleaning the Broken Star Café Bea moved to Lincoln to be closer to her son, Lionel. Of course, Lionel then took a job in Chicago and left his mother behind in a city where she hardly knew a soul. But Bea said she was settled and too old to move again. She decided to stay put. Her solution to loneliness was to write letters.

This is how Rick and Doris at the café found out about her mid-life crisis. Bea always began her letters with the same endearment:

Dear R and D,
It's August already. The marble bench I'm sitting on is cool through my cotton dress. I'm sure you'll think that's funny since I seldom sat down at the Star. I must be getting old. I've stopped at the Art Museum before going to work. As I entered the museum, the attendant at the door ignored me as usual. I suppose he sees I'm a harmless old biddy. As I write I'm sitting before a painting of a radiant white and honey-yellow flower so immense I feel drawn inside like a bee to nectar. I can almost feel myself

disappear into its petals. The identification plate below the picture reads:

White Iris, c. 1926
Oil on canvas
By Georgia O'Keeffe

I actually walked up close to the painting, my nose inches from the canvas. I almost felt like a giddy insect drawn to the center by a promise of sweet pollen. I suppose it's some kind of abstract foolishness. What was the artist thinking? It's not like any real flower I've ever seen. It's all petals. Where is the stem? Well, the museum bell just rang. I have to dash.

    Miss you as a duck misses water,
    Bea.

Bea grabbed her lunch sack and slipped quietly past the attendant. She was late and Mrs. McGinty would be waiting for her to clean. Bea walked the seven blocks to the wrought-iron gate and pushed the intercom.
"Who is it?"
"It's Bea."
Mrs. McGinty met her at the door.
"Sorry I'm late," said Bea. "I lost track of the time."
"I'm going out," said Mrs. McGinty. "You know what to do."
"Yes, Mrs. McGinty, I'll finish by four."
Mrs. McGinty snatched up her purse and was gone. Bea hurried to the kitchen. She placed her lunch sack on the table. After eating her sandwich, she gathered her cleaning supplies, scoured the sink and mopped the tile floor.

  Dear R and D,
    You won't believe what happened after I left the

museum. I finished cleaning Mrs. McGinty's kitchen and came to the living room. Now recall, this is the same day I saw the picture of the giant flower at the museum when I entered the living room I sucked in my breath.

Land sakes, I was surprised. There on the table near the front window stood the same flower. It had followed me to work. The iris stretched toward the sunlight like a fashionable lady in an evening dress. Three petals of her gown stood erect and three fell away. Do you believe in miracles? I bent to see the yellow blush at the center. I swear the iris turned toward me as if to speak. I jerked my head back. "Nonsense!" I said out loud. I backed away and began dusting. What do you think?

        Miss you both as a duck misses water,
        Bea

Doris folded the letter and placed it under the counter. She turned to Rick sitting on a stool having a cup of coffee. "Sometimes I think Bea spends too much time alone."

Rick raised his coffee cup. "She's a corker alright, but a good cleaning lady."

A week later Doris came to work and waved another letter at Rick behind the pick-up window. "I'll read it to you after we close."

Rick smiled and turned the eggs over on his griddle.

Dear R and D,

Well, I'll be darned if I didn't do the strangest thing. I'm almost ashamed to admit it. When I left Mrs. McGinty's that day after work, I saw more irises in the garden. I swear they hadn't been there before. I was sure something was going on with my head. I thought I was having one of those other-world experiences. I decided to walk the few blocks to the flower shop on the corner of 5th and Jamison St.

"Do you have irises?" I asked.

The clerk asked me how many I wanted. I told him only one and he wrapped a single iris in green paper. I felt a little foolish carrying it on the bus. On my way to my apartment wouldn't you know, there was Mr. Armstrong from the third floor. What an odd bird he is. Never says a word. I miss the friendly people of Turner's Grove. Well, anyway, I unlocked the door and carried the iris to the kitchen. I dug under the sink and found a coffee can. Oh my, I thought, this will never do. Would you believe, I placed the Iris in water, gathered my purse, and took a bus to Nagel's Department Store.

"Stuff and nonsense," you might say. Well, it may be, but I recalled Mrs. McGinty's beautiful vase and thought, my iris must have something at least as nice as Mrs. McGinty's. I found a lovely tall art-glass vase. It's slender and the light filters through iridescent green glass streaked with a lemon tint. It's perfect. It was worth the expense.

Miss you as a duck misses water,
Bea

Rick and Doris didn't hear from Bea for two weeks. It wasn't unusual. Bea was often forgetful. She'd always been dependable, but you never quite knew what she was thinking. Doris thought she grew more eccentric as she got older. The next letter came on a Saturday. Doris opened it after Rick looked the door at nine o'clock.

Dear R and D,

Maybe you're tired of my Iris saga. But I have to tell you how it's changing my life. It's like an evangelist was sent to call me to repentance. I can't believe it myself. But here it is. When I returned home with the beautiful vase from Nagel's Department Store, I placed Iris on the table. I sat on the sofa to admire the slender stem and velvet petals.

"Such a lovely lady in an evening dress," I said to myself. Then my eyes passed over the living room. How small and dingy it appeared. The slipcovers on the sofa reminded me of my own shapeless existence. The curtains, dark and tattered, contrasted dismally with the flower's natural beauty. The moisture rings on the coffee table were all of a sudden distasteful to me.

My thoughts turned to beautiful things. Why hadn't I thought about loveliness before? I suppose I was always working and simply accepted the ugliness in my daily routine. It began with the morning news. Because the world seemed messy and unkempt so did my life. Well, here's what I did next.

I moved the vase to the bedroom. I cleared the surface of the dresser and placed Iris in the center. I opened the curtains to let in more light. The brightness brought out the gloominess of the bedroom as it had in the living room. The tattered bedspread lay over a lumpy mattress. The permanent dark spot on the carpet stood out like a Rorschach blot. The second-hand dresser reminded me of a Sumo wrestler squatting on the floor. The iris seemed to droop in despair. I found my check book. Surely I can afford a few things, I thought. Well, have to run. There's cleaning to do. I'll write soon.

    Miss you as a duck misses water,
    Bea

What Bea told Rick and Doris later was that she woke early the next day. She placed the iris on the table and made tea and toast. While she ate breakfast Bea made a list: curtains, a small table for Iris. Do I dare think sofa? Why not dream? She added an area rug to the list and carried it into the bedroom. Bea scribbled 'bedroom curtains, bedspread, dressing table, area rug' on the paper.

She returned to the living room and poured a second cup of tea. "What do you think?" she said to Iris. Laughing at herself, Bea went on. "We deserve something more elegant than a shabby apartment. We'll fix it up a bit?

Bea dressed and hurried to the bus stop. At Nagel's Department Store she took the escalator to the top floor.

The next letter came to the Broken Star on a Monday morning. Doris was anxious to hear what Bea did next and read it as she had her first cup of coffee.

> Dear R and D,
> Well, there I was upstairs in the furniture department at Nagel's. I almost turned and ran. The sales-people's eyes watched me like I was about to shoplift a sofa or table lamp . My knuckles turned white from clutching my hand bag. I felt foolish in my plain dress. I stood in front of a showroom mirror and stared at my frizzy hair. "God," I said in half prayer. "What's happened to me? What am I doing in a place like this?" I was sure the salespeople had labeled me a frump with no cash.
> I turned over a price tag on the nearest table. Oh my, things have changed since I last bought furniture! I found a lovely cream sofa that would fit perfectly in my living room. A kitchen table in the next aisle would be perfect next to the window. I turned and admired a glass- top coffee table.
> "Can I help you?" asked a saleslady?"
> My land, she'd crept up on me like she wanted my scalp.
> I hesitated. "Well, I'm looking for a...," I mumbled. "Do you have a small table on which I might put a vase of flowers?"
> "I think so," said the saleslady. "I'll show you the one I like."

"I came by bus," said Bea. "Do you deliver?"

"Yes, we do. But there is a charge if the purchase is under $300. Over that amount, delivery is free," she said. You should have seen the expression on the woman's face. It clearly said I would not need free delivery. She led me to the other end of the showroom. The furniture was arranged on a beautiful area rug. At the end of the sofa was the perfect leaf-green end table.

"I'd like to buy that," I said.

The saleslady pulled the tag from the table. "This is $125.00," she said.

"That's fine," I said bravely. "And I'll take this area rug too. It reminds me of irises."

The sales-lady pulled the tag off the rug. "Are you sure?"

"Yes," I said confidently, trying to remember how much I had in my bank account. "There's a sofa I'd like sent as well."

The sale's lady began adding up the amount in her head. Her eyes seemed to twitch as if she'd awakened from wrong thinking. Which she was, of course.

I was having fun. I turned to the lady and said, "Follow me."

The sales lady pulled the tags as I indicated my purchases. At the counter I asked how soon my purchases could be delivered.

"Would Wednesday be alright?"

I paid with a check and asked her to point me to bedspreads and curtains? An hour later I staggered from the department store carrying my packages. I'd spent a great deal of money. But it felt so good. How nice the apartment will be for Iris."

                Miss you as a duck misses water,
                Bea

Doris folded the letter and replaced it in the envelope. She walked to the take-out window where Rick was getting ready for the morning rush.

"I think she's gone over the top," called Doris.

"Who?"

"Bea. A letter came this morning. You'll have to read it yourself during the break. It's a soap-opera."

The last letter they received, before Bea visited Turner's Grove, came at the end of the week.

By Wednesday evening Bea had arranged the new furniture, hung the curtains, and placed the area rugs. By now Iris had wilted. Bea removed the flower from the vase and placed the petals between the pages of her Bible. Bea left the apartment to buy a second iris. Returning home, she arranged Iris II in the slender vase and set it on the new side-table. She prepared dinner and set out her Goodwill china. Placing a candle in the center of the table, she looked over the room. "How lovely it looks," Bea explained in her letter.

> Dear R & D,
>
> I was exhausted after my furniture came. That night I carried Iris II to the bed room and set the vase on the new dressing table. The mirror reflected the flower's slender green stem and lily-white petals. It reminded me something. I moved quickly to the closet and lifted a box from the top shelf. I unfolded an emerald green night gown, a birthday present from my sister. I'd forgotten about it.
>
> "Now for a bath," I said to Iris II.
>
> I poured bubble-bath in the water. I hadn't done that in years. I soaked until the water cooled, toweled dry, and applied moisture cream. It felt so good. Maybe I shouldn't be writing this for Rick to read. I slipped the night-gown over my head. It fell luxuriously over my body. Returning

to the dressing table, I admired my reflection next to Iris II. Aren't I foolish for an old cleaning lady?

But it felt right. "Maybe I'll treat myself to a haircut this week," I said to Iris II. "Maybe I'll even buy myself a new dress." I laughed at my own generosity.

Here my adventure ends. I am going to slip between the fresh sheets and sleep peacefully.

"I haven't wilted yet."

                Miss you as a duck misses water,
                Bea

Faces From a Broken Star

CHAPTER NINETEEN

Twelve Lady Apostles

Thelma Larson, nee Burley, farmed the old Johnson place south of town. It was a beautiful spot along the river. Yet the farm was showing its age. Hidden beneath the foundations of the out-buildings, dry-rot was taking its toll.

Thelma and LeRoy had been married on the long side of thirty years. Dry-rot had also crept into their marriage. For Thelma, it came as loneliness. "Living with LeRoy," she told Doris at the Broken Star Café, "was like living in a black hole. If I lived in a well, at least I'd hear the drip, drip of water."

LeRoy babbled like spring run-off when they first married. Normally a shy man, he managed several hundred words in the beginning. He talked at meals and occasionally confided in Thelma about his dreams as they drank Ovaltine on winter evenings.

After marital routine set in, LeRoy's words began to fail. "I hardly noticed at first," said Thelma. "Each year LeRoy's sentences grew shorter and his words fewer. To tell the truth, the man has a dearth of words." Doris nodded sympathetically.

"Doris," said Thelma, "some days I stare across the table while he eats just to see if his mouth is working."

To be fair, LeRoy wasn't entirely mute. His managed "ah," "humph," "aha," "yup," and "yes'um" at the appropriate times. If LeRoy's words had babbled in the spring of their relationship, they were frozen by winter. Thelma felt alone.

The effect on Thelma was unnoticed by LeRoy. Thelma's best friend, Maxine, understood, she referred to LeRoy as "the post." Like the dry-rot in the out buildings, the silence didn't go away. Thelma found ways to cope. She began mumbling to herself in the mirror. She talked to herself at the kitchen sink. Strangest of all, she confided in the Twelve Lady Apostles.

The Lady Apostles were twelve Holstein milk cows who became her therapists. They stood in the tie-up and listened to every word Thelma spoke. Each Apostle's name, taken from the Bible, hung above her stall: Eve, Rebekah, Ruth, Naomi, Sara, Deborah, Delilah, Dorcus, Prisca, Mary, and The Other Mary, from Matthew's gospel. The most cantankerous milk cow was Jezebel.

It may seem sacrilegious to name cows after women in the Bible; but Thelma did it out of respect. She did not tell Rev. Urban at the New Revival church. Thelma knew he would never understand. Thelma simply loved the way the ladies listened with soft comforting sounds while munching their hay.

At milking time Thelma's voice mingled with the gentle chewing of the Twelve Lady Apostles. The ladies responded with an occasional Moooooo or smack of lips. In the tie-up Thelma talked about the roof leaking, her vacation plans, the declining attendance at church, and of course, LeRoy. She also told them of her recent indiscretion with Norman, the baker.

Norman was another solution to Thelma's pale existence and dearth of conversation. Thelma, in her late fifties, still turned a head or two. Perhaps LeRoy's initial interest in her figure had sparked his uncharacteristic conversation in the beginning.

Maxine, who knew Thelma in her twenties, said she could be mistaken for that dancer. The one who danced with Fred Astaire.

Thelma stared at Maxine, "You mean Ginger Rogers? Get out of here." Thelma pulled out her compact mirror for a peek. Her eyes sagged a little like other parts of her body. That could be blamed on thirty years of bending over milk pails.

Still, men in town did not ignore her as she walked down the street. Unfortunately, LeRoy's interest had tailed off to a slow drip from the faucet.

"I know, Eve, it's not right, Norman and me," Thelma said one day while milking. "I never thought it could happen." She continued to pull milk from her confidante. The first milk squirting into the bucket sounded metallic before turning to the familiar splash.

Rebekah was next in line. "Norman's a nice man." Squirt, squirt. "No, Rebecca, he isn't married. He's not cheating on anyone. I'd never stand for that." Rebekah turned her head, a puzzled gleam in her eye.

As the Lady Apostles stood in the tie-up, Thelma told of her affair with Norman. "LeRoy asked me one day why I was buying bread from the bakery. 'It's easier,' I said, 'and besides, they deliver on Wednesdays.'"

LeRoy, humphed into his coffee. Wednesday was LeRoy's day away. He drove his pickup to the Broken Star and then to Will's Feed Supply. From there he went to Presser for a Lodge meeting.

"Of course," Thelma said to Ruth one Wednesday morning, "I do miss Ladies' Aglow, but the Reverend Urban doesn't attend and doesn't know I miss. He's not much for lady's meetings." Ruth tried to kick the milk bucket. Thelma took no notice.

Wednesdays were a holiday for Thelma. She finished the milking quickly. In the house, she fixed LeRoy's breakfast. He'd eat lunch at Barney's Burgers in Pressor and dinner at the Lodge.

"You'll be home late tonight," said Thelma.

"Yup!"

"Well enjoy the meeting."

"Intend to."

"You won't drink and drive, LeRoy?"

"Nope."

As LeRoy drove from the house, Thelma climbed the stairs to run a bath. She poured Bubble-All in the water and had a dreamy soak. She rubbed body cream over herself. From the closet she selected a blue chiffon dress to accent her figure. Thelma turned from the mirror and decided to get another opinion.

She hurried to the barn and entered the tie-up on the opposite side. Parading up and down the barn, she showed the Lady Apostles her dress. "What do you think, Rebekah? Now, Delilah, you should know." Each cow turned bovine eyes to her voice. Thelma ran her hand over her breasts and down her hips. "I know I'm not young any more. I'm still attractive, don't you think?" Moooooo, came the reply.

Norman Grayson worked at Parker's Bakery in town. His specialty was cinnamon rolls, frosted with a mix of cream cheese, butter, confectioner's sugar, and vanilla extract. He rose at 4:00 a.m. in order to deliver fresh buns to the Broken Star Café. By three o'clock Norman's work day done and he had an urge to deliver bread to the old Johnson farm.

It was said that Norman smelled of sugar in the morning and sweet breads and pie crust in the afternoon. But never mind, he was a kind and sensitive man. He wasn't normally flirtatious. His affair with Thelma was a new experience for him. Actually, there was a strange affinity between them. If you could see Ginger Rogers in Thelma, it wasn't hard to imagine Norman as Fred Astaire with a mustache. Norman loved to dance.

At the farm Norman and Thelma sat at the kitchen table with coffee and cinnamon rolls. From there they moved to the living room and put Glen Miller on the phonograph. Thelma breathed in the scent of pie crust as if it were oxygen. They danced and danced until it seemed natural to climb the stairs to the bedroom.

"Oh Eve, it was heavenly" said Thelma in the tie-up the next day. "It's been so long sense I felt like this. Can it really be so wrong?" Thelma moved along the line of Apostles.

"Sara, I really think LeRoy is better because of it." Sara turned an eye to Thelma. "The way I see it, I'm happier around the house. LeRoy has noticed it. And he enjoys the fresh bread."

One Wednesday morning at the Broken Star Café, Doris poured LeRoy a cup of coffee. He sipped silently. On the stool next to him sat Tobias Strange, the barber.

"You've not been in for a haircut," said Tobias.

"Thelma's been cutting my hair. Haircuts are too expensive for the likes of me."

"They've been the same price for five years," said Tobias. "I can hardly keep the shop open."

"Humph." LeRoy blew over his coffee.

"You're getting deliveries from the bakery. Maybe that's where your money's going."

"What do you mean?"

"Every Wednesday I drive by your place, I notice the bakery truck parked in the drive."

"That's Thelma's idea. It's nothing to do with me."

"I'll bet not," winked Tobias.

If Wednesday afternoon meant a vacation to Thelma, the day was a hot oven to Norman. Since LeRoy stayed away late, Norman need not rush. It was lovely, a cup of fresh coffee with a cinnamon roll, dancing in the living room, and then a sweet roll of another kind upstairs.

For Thelma the best part was the conversation following their lovemaking. It was then Thelma knew she believed in God. Norman had been sent to her that she might have someone to talk to. After years of "ah," "humph," "aha," "yup," and "yes-um," and squinty eyes, it was the greatest gift. Norman listened to her. And unlike the Twelve Lady Apostles, who she loved dearly, he talked back.

But vacations in Florida do not last forever. The dream ended one Wednesday night as LeRoy drove home. Thelma was awakened early in the morning and told about LeRoy's fatal accident. Guilt swept over her. The Wednesday devils poked and prodded her conscience. Her stomach accused her of betrayal. She blamed herself and wanted to confess to Reverent Urban, but she couldn't lift the phone.

For days Thelma sat on the other side of the tie-up , staring into the liquid eyes of the Twelve Lady Apostles. They stared back sympathetically. She could not talk to them. She had acquired a dearth of words.

Norman called Thelma. When she did not answer, he drove to the farm. She would not see him. Guilt crept up her spine and threatened to topple her over. Norman finally gave up and moved to Lincoln.

Thelma returned to milking the twelve ladies. Milk pails continued to fill as she talked about her grief. "Oh Sara, I wish I'd done things differently. Maybe if we had gotten counseling, things could have been different." Sara munched her hay and listened until Thelma moved on down the tie-up.

One morning Thelma was talking to Jezebel about LeRoy. She felt that Jezebel, the meanest of all the Lady Apostles, understood. The cow turned her head and looked at Thelma as if to say, "Now dearie, get over it. The accident was not your fault. Life."

One afternoon Thelma heard a truck drive up the gravel road. She looked out the upstairs window and saw Norman step out of an old bakery van. She ran to the mirror, brushed her hair and checked her makeup.

News travels fast in Turner's Grove and it wasn't long before Doris heard from Maxine about her visit to see Thelma.

"It's the strangest thing," said Maxine. "When I got to the farm I saw the bakery van parked behind the barn. As I walked to the door I could hear Glen Miller's orchestra."

"Really," said Doris.

"Dance music was coming from the living room."

"What happened next?" asked Doris.

"I don't really know. I didn't dare knock. Then the music stopped. I stayed for several minutes. I heard nothing at all. There was a distinct dearth of words."

EPILOGUE

Blue Highways

Rick dropped the last travel bag in the back of the van. Returning to the house, he locked the door and ticked off his to-do list: neighbor's alerted, mail held, water shut off. He climbed into the driver's seat and stole a final look at the house.

At seven in the morning Main Street was just waking up. The lights of The Farm Supply spilled over into the parking lot. Rick parked the van across the street from the Broken Star with the motor running. The dark windows of the café held a reflection of his van. For thirty years customers parked between the diagonal lines in front of the café. *Not today*, thought Rick. *A piece of the town is missing.*

Rick grimaced at the closed sign. For a moment he imagined the jingle of the bell above the door. He could almost hear the swinging kitchen doors flap back and forth. He tried to recall Doris shouting good morning. He thought of Orlin, the Professor, Charlie and M. Celestine.

Rick reached in his pocket and pulled out a package of Life Savers. He popped one in his mouth and dropped the rest back in his shirt pocket. He glanced at the passenger seat and the book Doris had given him. For a moment the lights glazed again in the café. He saw the tables filled with people. The door opened. Laughter filled the street. Rick took a deep breath, pulled from the curb, and drove out of town.

Children's Books by the Author

The Mouse with Wheels in His Head
Fergus dreams of being the first mouse to ride the first Ferris Wheel at the 1893 World's Fair. But how is it to be done?

The Mouse Who Wanted to Fly
Fergus's second adventure takes him to Kitty Hawk where two brothers are going to fly the first airplane. Should a mouse be on the first flight? Fergus thinks so.

Mischievous Max, A Teddy Bear Story
Max Bear is not a cuddly Teddy Bear. His eyes are beastly and his fur is scratchy. No wonder Leon doesn't want to sleep with him. What if Leon takes Max to bed for just one night? Does he know Max Bear likes to do mischief in the night?

Fergus of Lighthouse Island
This Fergus is named after a great uncle who loved adventure. You may have met him as he rode the first Ferris Wheel and flew with the Wright Brothers at Kitty Hawk. But this Fergus isn't brave at all. He's not looking for adventure. But when a hurricane threatens Lighthouse Island, adventure finds him.

Cloud Climber (An Adventure for Seven to Ten Year Olds)
When Seth and Emily spend a few weeks with their grandparents, they're sure it will be the most boring weeks of their lives. But there is no time to be bored after discovering Three Friends Hill, the Banshee's Cave, and a treasure found in the hayloft of the old barn.

All books available at Amazon.com
or the author's website: genegbradbury.com

GENE G. BRADBURY writes from his home in the Pacific Northwest where he lives with his wife, Debbie. His writing encompasses poetry, short stories, children's stories and education material for adults.

Faces From a Broken Star is Gene's first book of short stories. His two books of poetry are *Traveling in Company* and *Quiet Places, Morning Walks: Notes Between Secular and Sacred*.

He has self-published five children's books: *The Mouse with Wheels in His Head, The Mouse Who Wanted to Fly, Fergus of Lighthouse Island, Mischievous Max: A Teddy Bear Story,* and *Cloud Climber*.

His work may be found in various children's magazines and adult periodicals. Gene teaches adult classes in theology in his area.

Gene has a B.A. in Philosophy, an M.Div. in Theology, and a Master's Degree in Spiritual Direction. Among his many interests he includes books and reading. He and Debbie collect books. A visit to their home is like a visit to a library. He is involved in numerous writers' workshops and enjoys sharing his stories during school visits.

Visit the writer's blog: scribblinglife.com

BookWilde Children's Books

Visit the author's website:
genegbradbury.com
and
writer's blog: scribblinglife.com

www.ingramcontent.com/pod-product-compliance
Lightning Source LLC
Chambersburg PA
CBHW031941070426
42450CB00005BA/310